THE HEALING SPIRIT

THE HEALING SPIRIT

Paul Tournier

Good News Publishers
Westchester, Illinois 60153

The Healing Spirit

This edition comprises previously
published material, newly revised,
updated and arranged from the GNP
editions of *The Healing of Persons* and *A Doctor's Casebook in the Light of the Bible*.

Printed in the United States of America.

Library of Congress catalog card number 79-88323
ISBN 0-89107-172-5

Contents

1
Treat the Patient, Not the Disease

"Man does not die," a doctor has remarked. "He kills himself."

God has a purpose for our lives, as for the world. And if the world is sick today because it is disobeying God's laws, men too are sick because they do not live in accordance with God's purpose. So the highest role of the doctor is to help men and women to discern what is God's purpose for their lives.

Every act of physical, psychological, or moral disobedience of God's purpose is wrong living, and has its inevitable consequences. Moreover, it compromises not only the health of the person who commits it, but also that of other persons, and that of his descendants.

"Treat the patient, not the disease" is the precept our masters teach us, and we are reminded of this need every day in our medical practice. Take two patients suffering from the same disease: one makes a rapid recovery, while the other is handicapped by some secret worry which has destroyed his will to live. But to treat the patient and not the disease means penetrating personal problems which patients often hide from us in order to keep them hidden from themselves.

I remember a young woman who was not one of my patients, but with whom both my wife and I had profound discussions on religious matters.

The child of divorced parents, she was beset by tremendous difficulties that stemmed from her mother's nervous state. She had a lively faith, but was wild, independent, and critical, and reacted by tensing herself against adversity. For many years she overworked, sleeping only a few hours every night, and cutting down on food in order to meet her financial burdens, in spite of signs of failure in her general condition.

When the lung infection revealed itself, she accepted it with her usual pluck, but without throttling her lively and independent spirit, and filled with pride when by some subterfuge she could disobey the doctor's orders.

As soon as she felt better she longed to return to an active and adventurous life, and accepted the demands of her treatment only in the hope of enjoying the compensations that such a future would afford.

I brought to this sick girl the Christian message of total acceptance of disease and of abdication before God of all self-will.

Just as my wife and I were leaving her room she called us back to say, in a voice filled with emotion: "You are right, what I need is to abdicate more thoroughly. I knew God was asking me to take some fresh step, but I did not know what it was."

Some time afterward she wrote to us: "I have truly accepted my illness—its spiritual as well as its physical suffering. There is no rebellion left in me. God has given me such peace that people have been asking what is the cause of the change and that has given me an opportunity to witness to my faith. . . ."

I do not need to dwell on the influence of personal problems on those who suffer from arthritic diseases. In these patients there is a mixture of hereditary factors traceable to wrong modes of life in previous generations and physical and moral factors.

Alongside overwork and lack of exercise is wrong eating: diets that contain too much meat or too many sweet foods, or that are too acid; or overuse of alcohol—in short, gluttony. In God's plan of creation there is a proper diet for man, and man cannot neglect it with impunity.

I know one patient whose doctor, aware of the part played by the psyche in her liver troubles, had recommended that she seek relaxation. For relaxation she listened to the radio. But this patient, who nursed in her heart a keen resentment against certain foreign statesmen, heard them making speeches on the radio and was so upset that she had another attack of her liver complaint. It is clear that the true solution would have been found not in "relaxation," but in being set free from the resentment that was poisoning her mind.

The same can be demonstrated in the case of phlebitis, which usually occurs in subjects who are physically and morally fatigued. I am thinking of a patient who was immobilized for several months by phlebitis. It was followed by pneumonia, a sure sign of the weakening of his powers of resistance. Nevertheless, the pneumonia healed rapidly, and the patient was convalescing very satisfactorily when the phlebitis recurred. This happened just when he was having a serious disagreement with his employer, who was thinking of dismissing him because of his long illness.

It would be very interesting to conduct systematic research into the moral problems of those who suffer from chronic skin diseases. The patient care of the doctor achieves some improvement, and then all at once, just when the victory seems to have been won, and without any obvious cause, the skin erupts again. Only rarely will the patient reveal to the doctor what is happening in his inner life at such moments.

These examples show the influence of personal problems. If this is so in the case of patients suffering from organic diseases, it is even greater in those afflicted by functional and psychical disturbances. The number of minor psychopathic conditions, of functional disturbances, of neuroses and psychoses has increased catastrophically over the last hundred years. Mental diseases by themselves are more numerous than all the other diseases put together. "This increase," says Dr. Alexis Carrel, "can be more dangerous for civilization than infectious diseases."

He senses that patients are not so much diseased as the victims of physical and moral disorders of their own lives and of the set in which they move. They have more need of advice than of remedies, but do not follow the advice he gives them. What they need is to find a spiritual axis for their lives rather than medical treatment.

The increase in nervous complaints is due to a general moral recession. This recession, with its consequences in family, professional, and social life, increases the number of problems that are due to marital, family, and social conflicts, to emotional shocks, to uncertainty and fear, to the falling off in honesty and trust, to worry and immorality.

Of these with nervous complaints, most are women, for it is the social and moral position of women that has undergone the most radical change during the last half-century. Formerly when a woman was married by her parents to a man whom she did not love or when she was the victim of the egotism and authoritarianism of a husband to whom she was a domestic servant, and who was unfaithful to her, she did indeed suffer, but she accepted her lot because the social conventions offered her no hope of escape. Nowadays she can contemplate divorce. And from the moment the idea occurs to her, her sufferings seem more unbearable, her conflicts with her husband become more serious, so that she finishes up suffering more acutely still. In a society governed by undisputed moral principles, life was relatively simple. Their collapse increases the number of moral "problems" in face of which the individual is left bewildered and powerless.

I wish to be very careful to avoid misunderstanding. We must not look for the restoration of social conventionalism which was often moral only on the surface. This formalism of principles, even when it appeared to accord with Christian teaching, was too much imbued with the spirit of the Pharisees against which Christ spoke.

Such formalism is not Christianity, but rather the negation of it. It was what crucified Christ. So then, if in this book I state my conviction that what the world and medicine stand most in need of today is a moral and spiritual renewal, this does not mean that I am advocating a return to the formalism of the beginning of the century, but rather the building of a new civilization in which the spirit of Christ will be the inner source of personal, family and social conduct.

The reader may suggest, however, that everybody comes up against difficulties in life—disappointments, remorse, injustice and conflicts—but everybody does not fall ill. The truth is that we all experience functional disturbances in varying degrees of intensity and persistence. If we examine closely the psychological reactions which are interfering with the normality of behavior in a neurotic, we are compelled to recognize that they are not different from our own, but merely more intense: They are still fear, jealousy, susceptibility, anger, dissimulation, self-pity, sentimentality, erotic desire, and depression. What characterizes the neurotic is the fact that the very intensity of his reactions sets up a vicious circle from which he is unable to escape on his own. His fear, for example, destroys his self-confidence, and his lack of confidence feeds his fear. He is afraid of himself, afraid of being ill, and it is this fear which is making him ill. The psychoanalysts have demonstrated that all the unconscious reactions of neurotics may be observed in the daily life of healthy persons. I entirely share their views on the continuity between the normal and the pathological in the case of psychoneuroses. All the behavior traits of the neurotic may be seen in our own false reactions to the problems of our lives. One goes a considerable way toward helping these sufferers in showing them frankly that one has reactions similar to theirs, since this removes their feeling of being different from others.

As a result of an insult, an injustice, a disappointment, we suffer from insomnia, anxiety, palpitations, displacement of affect, or overcompensation. In any case, these motor responses constitute a sort of self-treatment, an emotional discharge. Everyone knows that weeping brings relief. By means of this motor response, and also through the effect of the passing of time and through the instinctive forces of life and balance "gaining the upper hand," the reaction is gradually diminished. This is what I shall call the "minor liquidation" of the shock received, for rather than really healing it, it covers over the wound, to which the person becomes resigned.

It is by means of this "minor liquidation" that we neutralize the greatest number of our emotional shocks. But there is another course, which I shall call "major liquidation." It is the spiritual way. If we bring an insult or a disappointment to God, we can be delivered from it. What takes place then is a true liquidation, for then hate gives way to love, rebellion to acceptance.

If one looks closely into it, one realizes that there is no disease, however "physical," so to speak, which is not complicated with an element of neurosis. In her book *Servitude et grandeur de la maladie* Mme. France Pastorelli makes a penetrating analysis of the psychological complexes which are inevitably set up between the patient and those around him—the family, the nurse, and the doctor—and which can be resolved only on the spiritual level. It is impossible completely to avoid all affectation when faced with a sick person, whether it be the harshness of incomprehension, sentimental commiseration, calculated optimism, worried pessimism, veiled irritation, or helplessness. And the trouble is that every failure to act naturally brings into being an element of neurosis, which in its turn compromises the treatment and inhibits spontaneity.

My own experience is that in following Christ one can learn to be natural once more. He pointed this out when he said that in order to enter the kingdom of God one had to become like a child. It is characteristic of the child that he is natural. He can be natural even with people who are not being natural, and whom he thus helps to be natural again.

In communion with Christ the person suffering from nerves can rediscover the childlike mind, simple and uncomplicated; he can break the vicious circles of fear and rancor, and dare to show himself to others as he really is, without hiding his weaknesses.

In communion with Christ the doctor steps down from his scientist's pedestal, approaches his patient man to man, and is enabled to act naturally toward him.

The whole sense of this book is to show that a "medicine of the person" is made up of two methods. The scientific teaching of the medical faculty prepares the doctor well for the analytical study of the physicochemical, physiological, and psychological phenomena of man. There can be no question of doing without these techniques. I have often been consulted in recent years by students desirous of fitting themselves to practice a medicine of the person. I have always urged them to acquire during their years of medical training the most thorough scientific grounding the university can provide. But the doctor who wants really to understand men must add to this knowledge an experience of a spiritual nature. As Duhamel wrote, the doctor's art is essentially a "singular colloquy with the sick person," a confrontation of two who can understand each other on a spiritual level.

Man is not just a body and a mind. He is a spiritual being. It is impossible to know him if one disregards his deepest reality. This is indeed the daily experience of the doctor. No physiological or psychological analysis is sufficient to unravel the infinitely complex skein of a human life. The doctor sees how little his patients understand themselves, as long as they do not examine themselves before God; how apt they are to close their eyes to their own faults; how their good will is held back by circumstances, discouragement, and habit; how little effect his advice can have in reforming a person's life when the patient's mind is torn by an inner conflict.

When I decided to devote all my energies toward acquiring this deep knowledge of man, the first necessity was to give time to each of my patients, and in order to do so, to accept a smaller number. The way our profession has developed has had the effect of turning the modern doctor into a man in a hurry. Too many patients troop through his consulting rooms, generally without leaving the doctors time enough really to get to know them. The result is that patients see a doctor very frequently—or even a large number of doctors—without ever having time to seek the hidden cause behind the ills they suffer from. The diagnosis is arrived at after a clinical or radiological exploration, or a laboratory investigation. The patients are given advice and medicines. They recover successively from a number of illnesses. But why their resistance is weakened, why they have so many diseases in succession, why they lack the strength to live as they ought to live in order to be in good health, they only rarely have time to discuss with their doctors.

To understand a person's life, to help him to understand it himself, takes a long time.

Dr. Armand Vincent of Paris was asked to address a congress of doctors on the subject: "Towards a humane medicine." He began by quoting a remark made by one of his patients:

"We are prevented from dying," she had said; "we are not helped to live."

If we wish to practice a humane medicine we must answer that appeal. Then, inevitably, we are confronted by those questions which medical practice raises and to which science has no answer: What are life, death, man, nature, sickness and health?

Science analyzes phenomena but provides us with no clear, sure and general notion on these subjects. Medicine as taught in our faculties and textbooks remains silent on these. We turn, therefore, to the Bible, as Pascal invites us: "We know life and death only through Jesus Christ. Apart from Jesus Christ we know not what our life is, nor our death, nor God, nor ourselves. Thus, without the Scriptures, whose only object is Jesus Christ, we know nothing and can see but obscurity and confusion in the nature of God and in our own nature."

2
Looking for Meanings

Nature Speaks of God

To seek meanings and God's will does not spare us either from error or from doubt. Nor does it resolve all the mysteries of our destiny, all the insoluble problems which are sent us by any event in nature or in our lives. Nevertheless, it does give a new meaning to our lives.

We see this clearly in our patients. Patients who are sceptics endure a threefold suffering. They suffer from their disease, and they suffer on account of its meaninglessness for them. It is in their eyes nothing but a more or less serious vexation, the result of blind chance. They suffer again because it suspends their lives. They wait passively for their cure in order to begin living again.

The real believer, on the contrary, even though his faith may not deliver him from his disease or diminish the suffering it causes him, continues to live as intensely as before, and even more so. For to him life consists in seeking and listening to God. He can seek God in the silence of sickness as well as in the fire of action. His ears are open to what God says to him through his sickness, and that may sometimes be for him such a fruitful experience that he will bless his sickness.

The sceptic will be asking: "Do you claim that disease is sent by God? And if it does not come from God why do you want me to seek God's will in it?" His logic is impeccable but his triumph is sterile and the bitterness in his heart will compromise his recovery. The believer, on the other hand, is so absorbed in seeking what God means to say to him that he does not trouble to ask unanswerable questions.

In the biblical perspective, nature has a meaning. It speaks to us of God; not only of his greatness or his wisdom, but also of his love. The creation, according to the Bible, is a manifestation of the love of God. God created the world for love. Nature participates in the Fall and in the Redemption: "The whole creation," writes St. Paul, "groaneth and travaileth in pain" (Rom. 8:22); and in his vision of the end of the world St. John sees not only a new heaven appearing, but also a new earth (Rev. 21:1).

Modern man has largely lost the sense of his responsibility for his destiny. He feels himself hunted by external enemies, before whom he is reduced to running away or to waiting passively for help. This false attitude he owes chiefly to the conception of the world that he has gained from science. It has peopled his universe with blind, inexorable, automatic forces which prowl ceaselessly around him and in him: gravitation, chemical affinities, bacteria, heredity, and psychological complexes.

If he falls ill, it is because of his liver, or his blood pressure, the chromosomes of his parents, or the emotional shocks that he has suffered, the draft or the bacilli, which he happened to encounter. Against those misfortunes which befall him he waits for help that is itself external, foreign to him. He waits passively for technical medicine to attack them in its turn with irradiations, disinfectants, intravenous injections, or psychotherapy.

Thus the patient tends to become a battlefield on which formidable armies confront each other. A sort of armaments race takes place, and health seems to depend no longer on anything but the discovery of a bomb more powerful than the ones before it.

I was staying in Florence with a doctor friend. He called me to the bedside of an apparently moribund older woman. She lay there, her eyes vacant, making no more resistance to what was happening to her than would an inanimate object. She had passed through the hands of many doctors who had treated her heart with the powerful weapons of our various modern cardiac stimulants. My colleague leaned over her and said gently: "My dear, you must not rely only on medicine. There is yourself first, and God, and only after that the doctors." I saw in him the man of the people that he is, who knew how to talk to this woman of the people, recalling her to those basic truths whose importance is as great as ever in medicine, in spite of all our technical progress.

The patient looked in astonishment at this doctor, the first one to treat her as a person and not only as a case of heart trouble. She began to wake out of her passivity, to become once more aware of the part that she also had to play in the struggle. She was becoming a person again.

I do not wish to belittle the powerful weapons placed in our hands by medical progress and by the wonderful work done in the laboratories of our chemical factories. In this respect my generation has seen more changes than have taken place over several centuries. But everyone knows that it is dangerous suddenly to become very powerful.

Dr. Kressmann has rightly examined this question. He writes: "Yesterday I was seeing a doctor who described to me the tragic end of one of his patients who suffered from secondary carcinoma in the bone. Explaining to me that this youth of eighteen had received, since the age of nine, two injections a week of synthetic male hormone to promote growth, the practitioner concluded: 'It is difficult to know whether this intensive therapy contributed to the formation of the tumor, but I should not care to have prescribed it.' "

Dr. Kressmann continues: "Faced with the great mass of unknown quantities which we handle every day, I confess that I tremble at the carefree way in which our researchers nowadays advocate new methods, without giving a thought to their attendant risks."

Over against technical medicine which multiplies its doses, injections, interventions of all kinds, stand the naturist and homoeopathic schools of thought. Technical medicine, as we have seen, tends to make us regard nature as a world of enemies that must be attacked, coerced, and outwitted by every means at our disposal. The adherents of the second group, on the contrary, retain a sense of the organic links binding man to nature. They emphasize the wisdom of submission to the laws of nature, and the priority of hygiene and right living over aggressive therapeutics. In many respects their views are similar to those of the Bible which I am here discussing.

But in the absence of a firm biblical foundation there appears another danger, that of making nature herself a god so that naturism becomes a religion and an exceedingly fanatical one. Every doctor has seen its adepts who have become real slaves of their dogma. These two attitudes are not confined to healing, but can be seen in life in general.

The Bible, on the contrary, gives us a concept of nature and of man which alone can lead to completeness. For such a man the whole of nature is a gift of God; it is a book in which he may learn from his Creator the art of healthy living. But he has received from this same Creator power over nature so that he is not its prisoner. In the biblical perspective he takes his place in nature without being enslaved by it. Such also is the best tradition of medicine, a tradition which intoxication with modern discoveries is threatening to obliterate. The best clinical practitioners of every century have invariably drawn their inspiration from this tradition: careful observers of nature, always ready to be corrected by her, judicious in their prescriptions, bold when necessary, but having the patience of the peasant and no prejudices.

St. Paul also teaches this doctrine of liberty: "prove all things; hold fast that which is good" (I Thess. 5:21). "All things are lawful for me; but not all things are expedient. All things are lawful for me; but I will not be brought under the power of any" (I Cor. 6:12).

We see in the Bible that nature and society have a

meaning. They are God's instruments, but still only instruments. They speak to us of God and lead us to him. The men of the Bible heard in nature the voice of God.

Job heard God's voice in the tempest. An upright and God-fearing man, he had one loss after another, without complaining. First his cattle and asses, then his servants, his sheep and camels, and his sons and daughters. Thereupon he fell sick with "sore boils from the sole of his foot unto his crown" (Job 2:7). Lying on his mean pallet he had to put up with the sarcasms of his wife and the self-satisfied discourses of his friends! How vividly the Book of Job warns us against those unfitting and complacent sermons preached at the sick person's bedside; they make even biblical truths oppressive. Well might Job be roused to cry out in rebellion against God. But amid the roar of the storm Job heard the voice of God. Beside his majesty he saw how small man is: "Behold I am of small account" (Job 40:4).

Jesus Christ looked at the birds flying above him and the flowers in the fields around him and saw in them God's mighty care for each one of his creatures (Matt. 6:26). For him there is no such thing as chance. "The very hairs of your head are all numbered," he says (Matt. 10:30). With his disciples he watched the sunset, and taught them to discern "the signs of the times" (Matt. 16:2-3), the meaning of things, the meaning of history along with meaning of nature. He saw the sower in his field; he saw the parched grain that has fallen by the roadside and the wheat growing in the good ground (Luke 8:5); the flock of sheep that passed, following the voice of the shepherd

(John 10:4); the weeds growing in the cornfield (Matt. 13:29). Throughout the Bible men view God at work in natural events, and they seek to discover in them his purpose and his message.

In considering nature, there is nothing more important than noting that the Bible does not despise the human body. It calls it the temple of the Holy Spirit (I Cor. 6:19). "I will give thanks unto thee; for I am fearfully and wonderfully made," cries the Psalmist (Ps. 139:14). The supreme witness of God's love is the incarnation of Jesus Christ, in his taking the "likeness and fashion" of a man, with all the consequences, including suffering and death (Phil. 2:6-7). St. Paul compares the love of a man for his wife with that of Christ for his Church (Eph. 5:25). In the biblical perspective God's purpose is manifested in the harmony of nature as well as in the spiritual communion of souls.

St. Paul also wrote, "I buffet my body, and bring it into bondage: lest by any means, after that I have preached unto others, I myself should be rejected" (I Cor. 9:27). This text might be taken as a negative attitude toward the body, and an appeal to an ascetic mortification of the flesh, but I do not think it can be so interpreted. The Apostle has just alluded to the athlete who submits to a rigorous self-discipline in order to "keep fit." In his mind this severe training is not for a moment considered as an end, but as a means; not a redemptive mortification, but a proper mastery of the body for a particular purpose—the purpose of God in which this body has its proper role to perform. It is not a matter of treating the body as an enemy and raining blows upon it, but rather as a friend whom one helps to play his part correctly. As many doctors say, there is a hierarchy of the person in which the body is not opposed to the spirit, but subjected to it, as a good coachman holds his horse's reins firmly, not to maltreat it and paralyze it, but to put it on its mettle and to guide it.

In the privacy of my consulting room men and women of all ages have often told me that they believe in God's forgiveness for any sin except their sexual ones. For such sins they feel God can never forgive them, but only despise them for ever. In saying this they are projecting on to God their own contempt of themselves, and proving that this contempt is not due to the fact that they have sinned, but to the fact that the sin is a sexual one. How different is Christ's attitude! His greatest severity is reserved for those virtuous people the Pharisees. He openly defends before them the woman taken in adultery (John 8:3-11), and the challenge he throws out at them: "He that is without sin among you, let him first cast a stone at her" (John 8:7), shows how well he knows the human heart. Those are not the words of a man who has repressed his instincts into the subconscious! Jesus Christ did not marry, it is true. But we find in him none of the symptoms of infantile regression which are to the psychologist the distinctive marks of a repression of instinct. On the contrary, he shows astonishing virility. For those men are not the most virile who are weak enough to let themselves be driven this way and that by every instinctive impulse. The gentleness and confidence with which he speaks to this woman shows that his attitude is very far removed from that puritanical contempt of sex which is only too often thought to be biblical.

With regard to the harlot, Jesus said to his host, Simon the Pharisee: "Her sins which are many, are forgiven; for she loved much" (Luke 7:47). He does not deny her sins but unlike my patients of whom I spoke he does not consider them unforgivable.

The Bible honors sexual love; the Genesis account presents the establishment of sexuality by God as his crowning act of creation (Gen. 1:27; 2:18-24). After creating the heaven and the earth, then the animals, and finally man—"male and female," that is to say, undifferentiated—God invented sexual differentiation. A theologian once explained to me that the rib of Adam mentioned in this well-known story (my brother doctors will note that what took place was a surgical operation under anaesthesia!) could also mean "side" in its abstract sense; and that what happened was the separation of the masculine and the feminine principles, whose instinctive mutual search to reunite was to become a most fruitful source of spiritual development.

However intimate we are with a friend, or however close our spiritual communion with a fellow Christian, there always remains a last barrier of reserve which falls only in the marriage bond. The giving of the body in conjugal love is forcefully described by that bachelor, St. Paul: "The wife hath not power over her own body, but the husband; and likewise also the husband hath not power over his own body, but the wife" (I Cor. 7:4). In the biblical perspective this giving of the body in the marriage relationship, this tearing down of the last barrier of reserve is the symbol of the giving of the whole being and, finally, the symbol of the utter abandon of the self to God in faith. In speaking of the sex relationship the Bible uses the word "know:" "And the man knew Eve, his wife" (Gen. 4:1). "Joseph knew not Mary till she had brought forth a son: and he called his name Jesus" (Matt. 1:25). The Bible uses the same word for the supreme bond of faith which binds man to God: "And there hath not arisen a prophet since in Israel like unto Moses, whom the Lord knew face to face" (Deut. 34:10).

It may be objected that there are many Bible passages which speak of the incompatibility of flesh and spirit: "The mind of the flesh is death; but the mind of the spirit is life and peace" (Rom. 8:6; see also Rom. 8:5-8; John 6:63; Matt. 16:17; Rom. 13:4; Gal. 5:16-20, 24-5; I Tim. 4:8, etc.). As Dr. A. Schlemmer has explained, the word flesh which is used here does not mean the body but natural man in the totality of his person; body, mind, and soul. In the account of the Fall it is the whole man who cuts himself off from God by his sin. His physical disobedience (eating the fruit) and his mental disobedience (the woman incited by the serpent, and the man by the woman), are but the symbols of his spiritual disobedience—his claim to independence of his Creator. Similarly in the passages quoted the word spirit means the new man, regenerated by Christ, by the baptism of the Holy Spirit.

Note, for example, that when St. Paul enumerates the "works of the flesh" (Gal. 5:19-21) he includes not only what concerns the body (fornication, uncleanness, drunkenness, revelings) but also what concerns the soul and the mind: (lasciviousness, idolatry, sorcery, enmities, strife, jealousies, wraths, factions, divisions, heresies, envyings). Note also that though uncleanness is consummated in the body it obviously has its origin in the soul and mind. Similarly in the "fruit of the Spirit" which the Apostle then sets over against the works of the flesh he adds temperance, which has a direct bearing on the physical, to love, joy, peace, longsuffering, kindness, goodness, faithfulness, and meekness.

Life Comes From God

The lively force which sets in motion bodies and souls and things, and directs them on a fixed course, is life. The Bible tells us that all life comes from God. A patient of mine, the youngest daughter in a large family which the father found difficult to support, one day heard him mutter despairingly, referring to her, "We could have done without that one!" You can guess the effect of such a remark—not wanted by her parents, not wanted in life. She was overwhelmed by bitter anguish. Some years later she asked her pastor, "Can a child come into the world without God willing it?" The pastor answered: "You shouldn't be worrying about such things at your age. Run along and play with your friends." But that was precisely what she could not do for she felt herself to be different from the others. She believed herself to be unwanted. There are many people who feel to some degree unwanted. This is frequently the case with illegitimate children.

Our children are the fruit of the love which God has set in our hearts. The love we bear them is the reflection of the love that he bears them. That is our great responsibility. The child who doubts the love of his parents doubts the love of God. The child who thinks himself unwanted by his parents thinks himself unwanted by God.

One can easily imagine what effects such a feeling may have on the life force, on that vital energy which psychologists call the libido.

The only answer is given by the Bible—that all life comes from God. Nothing gives back such sufferers their self-confidence and the feeling of their own infinite value more than certainty that their life was willed by God, even if it is the fruit of some thoughtless sexual relationship between two drunken strangers on a night out. Their child is also a child of God. He owes his life not only to his parents but also to God who imparts his own creative power to men. Jesus Christ died for him too; he is the object of that special concern with which God favors the wretched. In the biblical perspective life is communion with God and death is separation from him.

"God likes life; He invented it!" I well remember these words, spoken by my friend Roger Faure, who gave his life for France while leading his battery in June, 1940. He often repeated it with that warm smile that lighted his face.

Throughout the Bible the idea of life is connected with God. It is portrayed as a force proceeding from the Creator and animating creatures. Life awakens at God's call. All through the story of the Creation we find the words: "God said . . . God said . . ."; it is the Word of God which gives life and existence to everything (Gen. 1:3).

Note that the fundamental distinction made by us

between the organic world and the inorganic world is scarcely present in the Bible. In the Bible there is but one world.

Every differentiation is a manifestation of life as understood by the Bible, right from the first separation of light from darkness (Gen. 1:4). Without God, all is nothingness, "waste and void" (Gen. 1:2). At God's call everything takes on movement and life. It is God who moves the stars; their infinite motions show forth the power of the life of God.

The Bible lays great stress on the superabundance of the life which God pours into the whole universe and which has made such a deep impression on biologists that they have spoken of the wastefulness of nature: "Thou openest thy hand, and satisfiest the desire of every living thing," cries the Psalmist (Ps. 145:16). But, as we see in the account of the Creation, there is a gradation. There is one life, but there are degrees of it, leading to that of man created "in the image of God" (Gen. 1:27)—that is to say, the life of man endowed through self-consciousness with a quality akin to that of God. And complete and total life is incarnate in Jesus Christ: "For it was the good pleasure of the Father that in him should all the fulness dwell" (Col. 1:19).

Observe men and consider that half-formulated subconscious thought which is, as it were, of the very texture of their souls. You will see that frequently, even in the case of believers, it is permeated by the idea of an opposition between God and life so that God appears to be a brake, or a barrier, limiting life. Men claim the right to "live their own lives" and in the name of that right they protest against the restrictive authority of God. It is as if God prevented us from living our lives when all the time it is only by him that we can live them to the full!

This same idea leads many believers to see God as the sort of father who systematically forbids his children everything that gives them pleasure and increases the joy of life. And so we come near to thinking that the life-force is opposed to God, whereas it was he who gave it to us. It is clear that to put it under lock and key is no answer. The solution is to abandon our life to God and to ask him to direct its powerful course.

"The Lord God formed man of the dust of the ground, and breathed into his nostrils the breath of life; and man became a living soul" (Gen. 2:7). A breath, let us note. The Bible gives us no static notion of life; it is presented as a compelling guiding force. The Bible does not consider spiritual life any more than it does biological life as having a separate existence of its own, like a sort of acquired capital. It is a motion from God animating and directing our souls.

Rather than physico-chemical mechanisms creating life it is actually life which directs these mechanisms and communicates to them their particular development to a definite end.

Dr. Jean de Rougemont has noted that in the most elementary of biological phenomena, the cell feeding itself, there is an element of choice. The cell chooses from its surroundings what it is able to assimilate and refuses the rest. Choice implies purpose. Dr. Tzanck uses this same word "choice" without which life is incomprehensible, and he says that everything takes place in biology as if an Intelligence inaccessible to our science had, in the beginning, imparted an impulse in a certain direction to the vital phenomena, which have since been unfolding according to a predetermined plan. With each of these constants there is a certain margin of normal oscillation which may be compared to the slight deviation from its course of a ship, thrust now to port, now to starboard, by the action of the waves. But like an automatic pilot correcting each deviation and bringing the ship back on to its course, this organic sensitivity insures constant regulation.

Neither does our spiritual life follow a straight line. It also is made up of perpetual oscillations. I often meet Christians who find this hard to accept. But it too has its regulator. Here it is the voice of God that plays the part of organic sensitivity. This voice of God in us we might call "spiritual sensitivity." There are the normal oscillations of doubt and temptation. And there are the more violent oscillations of disobedience to God, of sin.

This knowledge of God, this perpetual rediscovery of God with its new understanding of his will, even at the cost of our faults, is the meaning of life according to the Bible. In the fallen world the spiritual life is a cycle of sin and grace, of doubt and faith, of turning away from God and rediscovering him. As Calvin said "What is the end of man? To know God." And he added at once: "What is his happiness? The same." That is what gives meaning to life in general; but it is also what gives meaning to each thought, each feeling, and particularly to each action. As St.

Paul says: "Do all to the glory of God" (I Cor. 10:31).

Persons Are Spiritual Beings

The doctor's first task is to help men to fulfill their destiny, and that means helping them to become *persons* in every sense of the word.

What is the person? It is man in so far as he becomes adult, freed from himself because dependent on God, assuming full responsibility for himself before God. Such is man as the Bible presents him. This is what I now wish to show, emphasizing what it means for medicine.

In the biblical view man is not the most highly evolved of the animals; he is a special creation of God. He is not merely a physical and mental machine. He is spirit and soul and body for he has been created in the image and likeness of God (Gen. 1:26). The God of the Bible is a personal God who speaks personally to man, who calls upon him.

Throughout the Bible we see God calling men and drawing them out of the primitive mentality in which they were wallowing. It is a fact that the savage has no consciousness of himself as a person. He identifies himself with his tribe; he identifies himself also with nature by mystical participation. For him the microcosm that is himself and the macrocosm that is the world are confused.

"The Lord said unto Abram, Get thee out of thy country, and from thy kindred, and from thy father's house" (Gen. 12:1). God took Abram out of his tribe, out of his impersonal existence, conditioned by his environment. He made a person of him through his personal obedience to a personal command. The personal God makes man into a person. In the view of the Bible the link between God and man is a link between persons. It is this that makes man a complete being, responsible for himself before God. Right up to the last page of the Bible you will find men called by God out of the prejudices of their tribe, away from the impulses of their own instincts, so that they no longer live the automatic life of animals but become persons and prophets—prophets in the biblical sense but also prophets in the philosophical sense of which Bergson speaks—that is to say, emancipated, adult, creative, discerning the true meaning of things and teaching it to others.

God said to Moses, "I know thee by name" (Ex. 33:17). He said to Cyrus, "I am the Lord, which call thee by thy name" (Isa. 45:3). These texts express the essence of the personalism of the Bible. One is struck by the importance in it of proper names. When I was young I used to think they could well have been dropped from the biblical Canon. But I have since realized that these series of proper names bear witness to the fact that in the biblical perspective man is neither a thing nor an abstraction, neither a species nor an idea, that he is not a fraction of the mass as the Marxists see him, but that he is a person.

If I forget my patients' names, if I say to myself, "There's that gallbladder type or that consumptive that I saw the other day," I am more interested in their gallbladders or their lungs than in them as persons. The patient is at once aware of this. He realizes, of course, that the human memory has its limits, but if I am really interested in him as a person, his name will become important. He will be no longer merely a case to me—a combination of physical and psychological phenomena—but a person. By treating him as a person I help him to become one. This aspect of the doctor's task is particularly important today when man finds himself so gravely depersonalized by the mechanization of life and the "massification" of society.

This fact of the proper name symbolizing the person shows us clearly that the person is not to be considered as a body with a soul and a mind added, but as a complete entity in itself. In Genesis we read of God inviting man to give names to all the creatures (Gen. 2:19). This was the founding of science, but it also shows the creative power of man. Things become a reality. They can be distinguished only in so far as man gives them names.

In Switzerland the Federal Penal Code permits therapeutic abortion in exceptional cases and under strict medical control. For this purpose experts are appointed in each canton. One of these, a psychiatrist who lives near Berne, told us of an experience of his. A pregnant woman who was trying to get his consent to an abortion often referred to the child she had conceived as a "little collection of cells." Such is the conception that science gives us of man—a "little collection of cells," or, of an adult, a "big collection of cells." Instinctively this woman turned to science when she wished to devalue the life that was at stake. One day Dr. Plattner had the idea of putting to the woman this question: "What name would you give to this child if it were to be born?" At once the atmosphere of the conversation changed. The woman was silent. One felt that the child, as soon as she gave him a name in her own mind, was ceasing to be a "little collection of cells" in order to become a person. "It was staggering," concluded Dr. Plattner. "I felt as if I had been present at an act of creation."

Thus the doctor who puts himself inside the biblical perspective, who absorbs the biblical concept of man, becomes a doctor of the person. He no longer sees man as a collection of cells, but as a spiritual being, called to a personal destiny and endowed by God himself with priceless value. The parables of the Lost Sheep (Luke 15:3-7), of the Prodigal Son (Luke 15:11-32), and of the Good Samaritan (Luke 10:30-7) bear particular witness to God's personal care for every man, but the entire Bible is the reflection of it.

3
Persons and Their Problems

There is a mixture in a person's temperament of factors which come from God and factors which derive from wrong living. By means of prayer and meditation a man can distinguish what things in his temperament are God-given and must be accepted from what comes from wrong living and must be corrected. The study of temperaments opens up interesting perspectives into what might be called the medicine of the healthy.

"Prevention is better than cure," people say. And yet doctors rarely see the healthy. Most people go to the doctor only when they are afraid: afraid of disease, of infirmity, or of death. I have had an increasing number of physically healthy people coming to see me over the last few years. Their motives in coming to consult me were quite different. Some came because of their love of God, out of a desire to obey him and to devote to his service the best of their health and talents. They were seeking to know themselves better so as to organize their way of living in accordance with his will. It is a great joy to the doctor to be able to help a healthy person make himself healthier and to improve his usefulness to society. His sole aim is not to avoid disease, but to render better service. It is a great joy too for the doctor to meet a well-built man, full of possibilities. In our study and practice we rarely see such a man.

The choleric—energetic and domineering, imagining little but achieving much, seeing things as black and white rather than in shades of gray, insensitive and hardhearted, but leading a life of toil as severe on himself as on others, preferring quantity and speed to quality and depth—finds himself quite at home in this technological civilization. He occupies the positions of authority in political, economic, and even intellectual life, and imposes his faster temperamental rhythm on the social machine.

And so it is from among the sensitive, the artistic, the phlegmatic types that this society recruits its social misfits. The choleric sets the tone, and the conscientious but passive phlegmatic looks like a failure.

But in making human beings different, God meant each to have his equal place in society, and the present crisis in our civilization demonstrates that this elevation of the person of action to the rank of social norm can lead only to an impasse. All our effort and activity, all our standardization and organization end in political, economic, and psychological crises without precedent.

Too often creative imagination, calm thought, artistic production, the gentle things of life, the things of the heart and the soul have been strangled in this race to achieve and produce more and more. There is sterility amidst the granaries. For in a civilization in which action and technical progress have become the norm, money is king, and material return the only criterion of value.

Our mental hospitals are filled with people whose natures are artistic, gentle, and intuitive. They are crushed by the struggle to live, incapable of keeping up with the speed of the men of action, incapable of earning their living, defeated by the wounds inflicted on their sensitivity, stultified by their feelings of inferiority and social uselessness, discouraged and lacking faith in themselves. For though the phlegmatic is passive he is by no means insensitive—quite the contrary.

So then, one's temperament is a factor which, like everything he possesses, is neither good nor bad in itself. Each temperament has its dangers: authoritarianism in the choleric, negativism in the phlegmatic, daydreaming in the sanguine, and egoism in the melancholic. Each temperament has also its treasures.

The reason for our study of temperaments is that we may learn to know ourselves and what God wants of us. It is in order to submit and consecrate our temperament to God for him to use in accordance with his purpose.

Look anywhere in the Gospel story and you will see that those whose lives were decisively transformed through their contact with Christ belonged to the most varied categories of temperament: the shy and the impulsive, the humble and the proud, the practical and the intellectual. Alongside them, people of all classes of temperament—and among them many theologians fond of religious arguments—were able to brush past Christ without having any religious experience at all. They saw and heard the same but it got no further than the surface of their minds, and was never integrated into life. Therefore, while I stress the medical importance of a true decision for Christ, I do not want to confuse it with a sentimental inclination toward religion.

One might similarly think that confession would come more easily to an extrovert than to an introvert. The former, with his easy jovial manner, readily talks about himself. "The thing about me," he says, "is that I hide nothing. If anything, I am too frank." But this self-revelation is more apparent than real. It leads to no spiritual experience so long as it does not get beyond the flood of easy confidences to the thin trickle of real confessions. The problem of the human heart is the same for each of us, and is independent of temperament. The road to Christ is not easier for some than it is for others. It is difficult for all.

In the same way also optimism can be mistaken for faith. I am by nature optimistic, whereas my wife is pessimistic. I am confident, she is apprehensive. For a long time I reproached her for her pessimism as indicating lack of faith. For my own part I prided myself on my optimistic outlook as if it came from my faith and not from my inborn disposition. One day, when we both had a great act of faith to perform, I realized during my quiet time that I was being less than honest in confusing faith and optimism, to my own advantage. The truth was that real faith was as difficult for me as it was for my wife. And so I was much better able to help her to overcome by faith her natural pessimism than when I used to contrast it with my thoughtless optimism. It helped me also to see what was making my Christian witness sterile to timid and pessimistic people. As long as they felt that in what I said about faith there was more of a natural optimism than of real faith, they viewed it as "all right for confident people," but not for them.

The study of temperament ought to help us to live in accordance with our own true nature, to cultivate the talents which God has shared out to us, instead of comparing ourselves with other people, envying their gifts and being thrown into despair because we feel inferior to them. God loves each person equally and knows well that no one is more valuable than another.

It is of course between husband and wife that this mutual comparison is most frequently made and is most dangerous, for it leads to a progressive accentuation of the dominances of each temperament, which may eventually lead to what it is fashionable to call "incompatibility of temperament." Perhaps once more I can make myself clear by quoting my own experience, since this psychological phenomenon is not the monopoly of marriages that are "on the rocks." It is found in the happiest families. The more apprehensive my wife became, the more I tried to counterbalance her fears by adopting an air of confidence, even overdoing it sometimes, in order to cover up my own fears, for fear of encouraging hers. But the more confident I showed myself, the more my wife expressed her fears, in order to save me from falling into culpable overconfidence. The more advice she gave to the children, the more silent I became. And the more silent I was, the more advice she gave. One day she complained to me about my silence, and in my quiet time I saw that my behavior, instead of being regulated by a desire to obey the will of God, was in fact controlled by my natural temperament and my wish to counterbalance that of my wife. There was nothing to stop this vicious circle from growing worse and worse, unless it was broken by a change of attitude. And I saw at once that if I were to take my own responsibility toward the children more seriously, my wife would have an easier time with hers. Medical experience has taught me that there is no home that escapes this law of conjugal counterbalance. It manifests itself in a thousand different ways—loquacity and silence, expansiveness and reticence, optimism and pessimism, intellectualism and materialism, vivacity and gentleness, a love of solitude and a liking for society, conventionality and fantasy. It lies at the root of countless personal problems, or at least exacerbates them. It can lead to well-nigh insoluble marital conflicts.

Among all the personal problems to which I refer in this book, there is none which has greater effect on the physical and psychological health of mankind than marital conflicts.

The subject of sex sometimes causes the first breach in the complete confidence existing between children and parents and erects moral barriers between them because parents have not found the solution to their own sex difficulties. Sometimes their complete silence leaves the child a prey to unhealthy curiosity, and often to exhausting masturbation, followed by precocious sexual abuses. In this way young people, through having made a bad beginning in their sex life, spoil their happiness forever. On the other hand, sometimes parents approach the subject in a spirit of conventional moralism which presents the whole subject of sex as sinful. They say nothing of its divine aspect, set up countless stubborn complexes, and plunge the young into a sterile and obsessive struggle against impurity which is as exhausting as sexual abuse, and undermines their confidence in themselves.

And then there are all those unmarried people who never succeed in developing their personalities to the full because they never manage to come to terms with celibacy, while others, whether married or not, ruin their health in sexual excess. And there is the lifelong wearing down of physical and moral resistance by unreal imaginations, unhealthy reading, sexual selfishness, and the double life led by so many married people whose secret guilt prevents them from discovering the tonic force of true sexual harmony. Doctors know how few men and women enjoy the physical and psychical powers which full and proper sexual development can bring.

Marital conflicts are even more difficult when it is the woman who is the stronger of the two. I mean strong not only in character but also in virtue. Among the couples who have come to me over the last few years, I could point to many whose problems are basically similar.

Strong wives are thus constantly called upon to try and cope with the difficulties brought about by their husbands' weakness, acting in their place, paying their debts, and taking complete control, so that their lives are a continual burden.

Saint Paul remarks on how difficult the strong find it to understand the weak. A miracle from God is needed. I have seen it happen in a sufficiently large number of cases to be able to affirm here that God has a solution to all these conflicts. But I have known also of sufficient failures not to underestimate the difficulties, and to know that apart from a miracle from God there is no answer to these marital vicious circles.

It is only when a husband and wife pray together before God that they find the secret of true harmony, that the difference in their temperaments, their ideas, and their tastes enriches their home instead of endangering it. There will be no further question of one imposing his will on the other, or of the other giving in for the sake of peace. Instead, they will together seek God's will, which alone will ensure that each will be able fully to develop his personality.

In every argument between a husband and wife there are apparent causes: conflicting ideas, opinions, ideals, and tastes. But behind these apparent causes there are real ones: lack of love, touchiness, fear, jealousy, self-centeredness, impurity, and lack of sincerity. Indeed, one may say that there are no marital problems; there are only individual problems. When each marriage partner seeks quietly, before God, to see his own faults, to recognize his sin, and ask the forgiveness of the other, marital problems are no more.

Most of all, a couple rediscovers complete mutual confidence, because, in meditating and in prayer together, they learn to become absolutely honest with each other.

Such honesty is very difficult to achieve. One always feels that if one makes a total confession, if one reveals all one's secret thoughts, one must lose the confidence of one's partner forever. The truth is quite the contrary. A union founded on complete mutual frankness is notably more solid than one which is thought to be safeguarded by prudent reservations. This is the price to be paid if a man and a woman are to cease living side by side like strangers, to come out of their spiritual solitude and create a climate of normal mental life.

This is the price to be paid if partners very different from each other are to combine their gifts instead of setting them against each other.

Christianity consists in forgiving even those who do not come to us and eat humble pie. Following in Christ's footsteps, far from abasing us, ennobles us.

I have not mentioned conflict between a child and an unjust teacher. But then I could not possibly list all the conflicts which spoil lives. There are all those connected with work—not only between employers and employees, but more often still between foremen and workmen, between jealous workmen, between competing employers. And there are all the social, political, and international conflicts. There, as in the family, only a return to God can bring a true solution—reconciliation between employer and employee, between competitors, between political opponents, between nations, and between races.

Personal problems are interconnected like the links in a chain. A matrimonial conflict, for example, may bring in its train rebelliousness, laxity, alcoholism, and dishonesty. For when a man does not feel strong enough, when he despairs of solving some vital problem in his life, he tries instinctively to conceal his defeat by running away. And this flight creates a new problem which makes setting right his life more difficult still. Sometimes he is aware of this, but more often flight is unconscious.

There is flight into dreams. Real life is harsh. It is constantly injuring our sensibilities. The temptation to escape from it by flight is the stronger the more sensitive we are. We run away in order to protect our sensitivity, to escape the conflict which wounds it. The land of dreams is close at hand, so that one can escape into it at any moment, far from these painful realities. The escape often takes the form of a continuous story, a novel in many episodes which a person tells himself, going over the episodes again and again, and which absorbs his mental energy. It is a secret treasure into which he pours the best of himself. It is his way of turning the tables on harsh reality. He composes for himself a life in which he is always winning victories, and this compensates for the defeats he sustains in real life. In his fantasy he always plays the star part, he is always loved, esteemed, understood; he is always in command, he is free to sacrifice himself nobly.

The sort of dream of which I am speaking here is sterile and ineffective. It is fatiguing rather than restful. Above all, it aggravates the divorce between the ideal and the real. We are the more ready to take flight on the wings of dreams the more mediocre reality is, and reality seems the more mediocre the more we compare it with some idealistic dream.

There is also flight into the past. Many people have

their eyes turned constantly backward. They relive their Golden Age, a distant era in which they were happier, amid successes and joys. In this way they escape from the problems of the present, which they no longer try to solve, and savor the joys of the past.

Moreover, not only joys are involved. Regret and remorse can act equally dangerously as a flight into the past. The scrupulous mind which is constantly going over the past, taking a somber pleasure in analyzing it, is escaping into unreality quite as surely as the one who goes back to its brighter pages. For the center of gravity of a person's life to be behind him is the opposite of true living, which is a march forward. Thus a person's existence becomes sterile and incapable of providing solutions for his problems.

And then there is flight into the future. Escaping into the future, constantly making plans, is another form of flight into dreams, another way of escaping from the imperfections of the present. In its extreme form it becomes what is called the flight of ideas. Thought follows thought in such rapid succession, jumping continually ahead, that they become ineffective, leading to no sustained action.

I used to have a tendency toward living in the future. I was always forming fresh projects which seemed to me to be finer than what I was engaged at the time. My wife, on the other hand, lived in the past. She enjoyed a journey after it was over, when she could be certain that no unforseen event would spoil it. Happily, we have met together in the present, to live truly together.

Living with God means living the present hour

which he gives us, putting our whole heart into what he expects of us in that hour, and leaving the past and the future to him, to whom they belong.

The reader will have some idea of how much might be said about flight into disease. The fact is too common and well known for me to need to dwell on it. No one escapes it. Time and time again in my own case, self-examination has shown that a sudden feeling of fatigue, a headache, or an attack of indigestion is really a trick played on me by my own unconscious. A difficulty or a disappointment had interrupted the smooth flow of my work; a difficult letter to write, a puzzling case to sort out, or a disagreeable task to be undertaken had held me up, and so my unconscious was furnishing me with a good excuse for postponing it. All functional disturbances and, a fortiori, all neuroses, may be seen to involve a secret flight into disease. This, of course, is not to say that the disease is therefore "imaginary." A serious injustice is done to people suffering from such disturbances if they are accused of inventing their troubles as an easy means of escape. The feeling of not being understood, of not having their troubles taken seriously, from which they so frequently suffer, prevents these people from coming out of their unconscious refuge. In order to be able to come out of the tiny shelter that they have built against the storms of life, they need to feel that they are understood, loved, and supported.

Mention must be made now of what may be called "noble flights." Addictions are not the only form of flight. Often some of the best things we do in this world are an escape.

I am thinking of art and of science. I know some scientists whose devotion to their work is wonderfully conscientious and fruitful. Nevertheless their work is a form of escape, compensation for a family life which is not a success. I am reminded of a man who told me that his life began when he went from his house to his artist's studio, and that it stopped again, in a sort of parenthesis, whenever he locked up his studio. How many studios and laboratories act in this way as an escape world where we try to forget the reality outside which we do not know how to cope with?

I cannot close the list without referring to the most troublesome flight of all—flight into religion. The religious life itself can be an escape—an escape into a little mystic chapel which is like an island cut off from the world, where one can hide in order to escape the world and its wounds. It is possible also to use the active and intellectual side of religion as an escape. I know myself how I have taken pleasure in theological arguments at which my mind was more flatteringly successful than it was in tackling the practical, concrete problems of my life.

Western society is dominated and governed by noise, newspapers, radio, and speed, so that men have lost the sense of meditation, of mature reflection, and thoughtful action. But all this feverish activity is also a form of flight, by means of which men are trying to cover up their uneasiness, their spiritual emptiness, defeats, and rebellion.

A disciplined life in all spheres is one of the important conditions of physical and psychic health. Every day doctors have to deal with people who are worn out and unable to stand up to the life they lead. They generally assert that it is impossible to alter the way they live, and sincerely believe that their overwork is the product of circumstances, whereas it is bound up with their own intimate problems.

There seems to be a law of inertia in the psychological and physiological sphere, as there is in the realm of matter. On the one hand, a person who is run down may retain for a long time the appearance of health, while the balance of his strength is definitely in deficit. And on the other hand, when improvement in his condition begins he does not at first feel any amelioration. He retains a deceptive look of exhaustion which has to do largely with the destruction of his self-confidence. There is a sort of deferment of effect in both directions. It is as difficult to make a person who is overtaxing himself understand that the strength he thinks he has at his disposal is no longer anything but a facade as it is to make him realize, when he has cracked under the strain, that he could now take up some form of activity again, although he feels himself to be still in a state of exhaustion.

There are more intellectual and spiritual gluttons than one might think—that is to say, people who make excessive and undisciplined use even of the best things. I am thinking at the moment of a friend with whom I had conversations over a period of several months. He was a Jew. He was seeking Christ. But our long discussions were getting us nowhere. One day he came back to see me and told me he had found Christ. He had met a Christian who had simply told him that he was an intellectual glutton. Examining his conscience, he had suddenly seen that his inexhaustible religious discussions, however interesting they might be, were nothing but a kind of intemperance, and that they were blocking the road to his conversion.

Speaking of God's purpose for the normal life of man, Carton formulates what he calls "the law of the three rests." First there is the annual rest, the example of which is given us by nature, which rests during winter. It is possible that winter holidays are more beneficial than those taken in summer. At the time when insolation is such that we are deprived of part of the sun's energy, a few weeks in the mountains—in the snow with its strong ultra-violet irradiations—would without doubt be the best kind of holiday, and perhaps the day will come when the educational authorities will realize this. As early as the fifth century B.C. Hippocrates was recommending the reduction of activity and of food during the winter—he even prescribed only one meal a day!—in order to conform with the law of nature.

Next is the weekly rest, laid down in the Bible. Here again it is scarcely necessary to point out the constant misuse of Sunday, a day on which many people fatigue themselves even more than on weekdays.

Lastly there is the nocturnal rest, the importance of which was understood by Christ himself, and which our civilization has so drastically reduced with the perfecting of artificial lighting.

I need not stress the part played by worry, interior and exterior conflicts, temptations to impurity, fear, and ambition in this question of sleep.

I can remember my astonishment and even my indignation as a doctor, on hearing a lady remark, a few years ago, that insomnia was a symptom of sin. My experience of these last few years has led me to realize how much truth there is in this assertion. Doubtless there are exceptions, nor is the relation always direct; and it would be wrong to suggest that a person who sleeps well is less sinful than one who suffers from insomnia. But I cannot keep count of the number of patients I have seen rediscover the habit of sleep as a result of the transformation of their lives brought about by submission to Jesus Christ.

It is the quality of sleep which is changed as much as anything. Here is what one patient writes: "Sleeping less, I rest more, because my nights are absolutely calm now that my life belongs entirely to God. I sleep for about seven hours. Often less. I have learned to sleep in the afternoon when I have a moment's opportunity. My conviction is that God gives us complete directions for our physical life if we put ourselves entirely in his hands."

The opposite of flight into overwork is flight into passivity, withdrawal, negativism, and idleness. Laziness has considerable importance in medicine. Many people, even apparently very active people, are lazy in that they exert themselves only as much as they find agreeable. Thus, for example, while engaging in intense intellectual activity they neglect all forms of physical exercise.

It is laziness which prevents so many people from rising early so as to have enough time for prayer before the day's work and entering upon it zealously and joyfully. It is laziness which ties up so many people in unsociable, narrow, distant lives, deprived of the continual social exchange which is the law of human life.

Lack of exercise is one of the commonest physical shortcomings. Its consequences on the health of the body are well known: obesity and plethora of the sedentary.

Order can of course be a personal problem, when it is so rigid and fussy that it is thought of as the most important thing in life. But disorder is also a problem, and one that is particularly harmful to the atmosphere of a person's life. I know something about this myself. I have a lot to do in this respect because I am untidy by nature. One day I saw that I had no right to suggest to others that they should put their lives in order when I myself had so many cupboards in disorder, letters unanswered, and unread medical journals piling up. When I said something of this to my son, he told me that he would pray that God would give me the strength and perseverance necessary for this work. But on the following day he came back to talk to me about it. He had thought that he would help me even more by tidying up his own room to encourage me. Over a period of several months I gave up a number of other activities in order to get myself up to date, and it was a great liberation.

Indiscipline is closely related to laziness and disorder. Charles was a man whom I got to know while he was unemployed. He had lost his job as a result of illness, and his heart was full of bitter resentment against social injustice. We had quite a lively discussion.

But three months later Charles, still unemployed, was in my consulting room again. He told me what had happened to him. During a walk in the mountains he had suddenly thought himself lost. At that moment the memory of the evening spent with me, and especially the memory of the serene joy of another unemployed man, had come to him. He had started to pray. His adventure ended without mishap, but as he came back down the mountain he had thought seriously over his own life. He was dissatisfied with himself and wanted to live the clear, confident life of which we had spoken. But he did not know how to go about it.

I told him what my own experience had been. Then he started to tell me of all the moral indiscipline to which the distress of unemployment had opened the door. I had a new man in front of me: no longer the victim blaming society, but the sinner acknowledging his guilt. While he laid his faults before me, I considered how great a moral danger the idleness of unemployment is for those who are lacking in culture and in depth of spiritual life. His wife, a militant Communist, had a job. And he, in his long empty day, could no longer even summon up enough energy to light the fire for dinner. His wife was threatening him with divorce, and their home was nothing but an arena for violent quarrels.

When he left me he said that he intended to get up early, begin his day with a period of meditation, and then take some exercise and do the housework. His wife was astonished when, the next day at noon, she found the flat tidied up and the lunch ready.

A few weeks later he was a quite different man,

tidily dressed, disciplined, cheerful, and friendly. His home was happy and he soon found work.

At Christmas time I made the acquaintance of his wife. It was the first Christian festival she had taken part in since her childhood. She burst into tears when she heard her husband saying what God had done in his life and in his home. She made friends with my wife, and unburdened herself to her.

One day two years later Charles came to me, very upset. He told me at once that he had been backsliding, that for some time he had given up meditation and prayer. Temptations had come, and he had spent money which had been entrusted to him, and which he had now to pay back. He needed some money in order to get himself out of trouble. It was obvious what he had come for.

But I knew that what he really needed was a fresh experience of God's grace, rather than to get off lightly. I told him calmly: "You are going to see your employer, Charles, and to tell him what you have done."

"But that means prison!" he exclaimed.

I chanced to meet him in the street next day. He was beaming. He came toward me eagerly. He had spent a terrible night, but he had finally been able to pray. His employer had received him quite differently from what he expected, and had proposed that he should repay the money in monthly installments. Now he was determined to be disciplined.

4
Life's Enemies

Death and Disease

The fear of death plays a much larger part than we imagine in many of our patients, even in those who seem to be the strongest. How valuable it is for them to be able to speak to us about it and also for us to speak about it to them! It happens too seldom.

There is an old man, distressed and embittered, whom I have been seeing for several weeks without being able to feel that my visits have done him any good. He always brings out the same bitter complaints about his loneliness and his failing faculties. And he adds tragically: "I have always found fault with people; I have always wanted affection but I repel everyone with my surliness." On one occasion after a long silence he suddenly began to talk to me about his fear of death. "I've been obsessed with it all my life," he said. "When I was just a child I used to hang around the cemetery, overcome with emotion. I would hide when I saw a hearse and yet it fascinated me. Now that I am old the fear is worse than ever."

As he spoke a small voice deep inside of me was

saying: "You must pray with him today." But I hesitated. How would he take my suggestion? Had he not just been regaling me with all his criticisms of the Church, of the pastors who had done him harm, and with all sorts of intellectual objections to faith? And then we always find it difficult to suggest to someone, quite simply, that he should say his prayers.

I made the suggestion, and he replied: "I wanted it so badly but I didn't dare to ask you. As I have told you, I am an unbeliever, but I am in torment. After your last visit I tried to open the Bible but what I read repelled me. Then on Sunday I wanted to listen to a sermon on the radio, but what the preacher said disgusted me and I switched it off. Yes, thank you, will you pray with me?"

I write these lines with diffidence. Perhaps with death more than with anything else we feel that faith consists in respecting God's mysteries rather than in trying to explain them. And yet God can teach us through the Bible, for what we think about death is of great importance to our patients even if we do not speak to them about it at all.

I must attempt to set down the biblical view of death, and in doing so I follow Professor Jacques Courvoisier's study. "In Christian doctrine," he writes, "death . . . does not figure as the end of a normal process but as the result of a state of things disordered from the beginning." The order established by the Creator was indispensable to life; man's violation of it, therefore, necessarily leads to his death. But in his mercy God delays this outcome. He comes to man's aid. He heals his wounds. He protects him in spite of himself against the dangers into which he has run. In short, he grants him a respite and in this respite our life is situated. The doctor, even the non-Christian one, is in this sense God's fellow worker: he helps to retard death, to prolong this "respite of debt," during which a person may find Jesus Christ and receive through faith the promise of forgiveness, of victory over death, and of resurrection.

The first point is that the world created by God was perfect. At the end of the account of the Creation we read: "And God saw everything that he had made, and, behold, it was very good" (Gen. 1:31). In Psalm 19 in which the poet sings of the wonders of nature, he adds: "The law of the Lord is perfect" (Ps. 19:7). That does not mean only the moral law but also the order instituted in nature by God in the beginning. The central idea of the Bible is that this original order has been upset by man's disobedience so that the world in which we live and our own nature are "out of order." Consequently we are doomed to die. The reestablishment of order is only possible if God intervenes once more and this he does in history in accordance with his purpose. God's intervention begins his covenant with the people of Israel, is continued in the ministry, death, and resurrection of Jesus Christ, in the history of the Church, and will be consummated in Christ's return.

The world in which we are living is very different from the perfect world willed and created by God. It is a fallen, tainted world. This is stated in the well-known account in Genesis, and the view taken there persists throughout the Bible. "And the Lord God took the man, and put him into the garden of Eden to dress it and to keep it. And the Lord God commanded the man, saying, Of every tree of the garden thou mayest freely eat" (Gen. 2:15-16). So in this primitive order God gave man his work and his food.

The story continues, "But of the tree of the knowledge of good and evil, thou shalt not eat of it, for in the day that thou eatest thereof thou shalt surely die" (Gen. 2:17). We know how the serpent came and said to the woman: "Ye shall not surely die: for God doth know that in the day that ye eat thereof, then your eyes shall be opened and ye shall be as God, knowing good and evil" (Gen. 3:4-5). According to the Bible then, evil and death do not come from God. God actually sought to preserve man from them by requiring of him strict submission to the perfect order of life. Man's disobedience is his claim to be his own god, to judge good and evil for himself, to conduct his own life. Thus he cuts himself off from God, disturbs the perfect order, and the inevitable consequence is death.

Professor Ellul, who is a lawyer as well as a theologian, has pointed out that we have here not a punishment meted out by God but a "sanction" by which he means an unavoidable consequence of man's behavior. The sentence, "In the day that thou eatest thereof thou shalt surely die" at once appears less as a threat than as a warning. It is like a notice giving warning that it is dangerous to touch high-tension cables: the sanction is death. Verses 17 to 19 of this chapter of Genesis show that the sanction is also physical and social suffering symbolized by the pains of childbirth and by the difficulty man will have in earning his bread.

The suffering of man is also the suffering of God. That is my reply to those who tell me that they can't believe in God in the face of all the suffering that goes on in the world. The state of the world causes God so much suffering that we are told that "it repented the Lord that he had made man on the earth, and it grieved him at his heart" (Gen. 6:6). Throughout the Bible evil and death are the enemies of God. "The devil," we read, "that had the power of death" (Heb. 2:14), a power hostile to God which he will annihilate in the end. "Death and Hades were cast into the lake of fire. This is the second death, even the lake of fire" (Rev. 20:14)—that is to say, the death of death.

God's warning, "In the day that thou eatest thereof thou shalt surely die," may seem to contradict the idea of a respite discussed earlier in the chapter, but there is a double aspect of death— spiritual death as well as physiological death. The moment man disobeys he cuts himself off from God. This is sin resulting in spiritual death. Sin is everything that separates from God and from our fellow men. But the two aspects of death are inseparable: spiritual death, entering into man, will be manifested sooner or later in his physiological death.

In this respect, experiments in the artificial culture of living tissues carried out by Carrel and his pupils have revolutionized our ideas. Previously it had been thought that, from the scientific point of view, we should die because we were made of organic tissues that were destined to die, that it was the death of the parts that brought about the death of the organism as a whole. Such is by no means the case since these parts, suitably cultivated, can continue to live indefinitely beyond the time that they would have died if left in the organism. It is therefore the destiny of the organism as a whole that governs the death of the parts.

The mystery of that destiny remains. Why did man, having been created perfect, cut himself off from God, compromising his own life? I shall return later to the problem of the connection between sin and disease, but the biblical perspective shows that we cannot understand the whole of God's mysteries. I hope, however, that I have helped some to understand better such Bible passages as: "The wages of sin is death" (Rom. 6:23); "servants . . . of sin unto death" (Rom. 6:16); "the sin, when it is full-grown, bringeth forth death" (Jas. 1:15); "Therefore, as through one man sin entered into the world, and death through sin; and so death passed unto all men, for that all sinned" (Rom. 5:12).

Continuing we find that the first consequence of this separation from God is fear (Gen. 3:9-13). Adam hid among the trees. In passing it may be worthwhile for us to ask ourselves what are the trees behind which we hide in order to escape our insecurity or our moral responsibility. They range from our university degrees and our reputation to the state of our poor health. As we hide God calls us as he called Adam: "Where art thou?" Adam replied: "I was afraid, because I was naked."

This reference to Adam and Eve becoming aware of their nakedness has an obvious sexual significance. But, as I showed earlier, those whose psychological complexes incline them to exaggerate the importance of sexual sin see this interpretation only. They identify the biblical idea of original sin with the sex instinct. The truth is that this story clearly shows that it is because of his spiritual separation from God that man has got into difficulties, in sexual matters as in every other sphere.

To me the word "naked" here seems to mean equally "unprotected." In wishing to be his own god, man discovers his weakness and insecurity; in wishing to judge for himself how to use the power God had given him, he becomes aware of the disasters he risks. Look how "naked" men feel in regard to the atomic bomb! Dr. Stocker sees yet another meaning in this nakedness. For him, it is the nakedness of the soul which has lost salvation. That is why, he adds, when we find salvation again we can speak of being "clothed" with it.

The insecurity of a person's life is underlined especially by disease. "Disease is a sign of the death which is to come," writes Professor Courvoisier. "Every disease has in it the germ of death." Doctors at any rate will not contradict him! Although in health men repress as far as they can their terror of death it reappears with the slightest disease. When, in our consulting rooms, they ask us in as detached a tone of voice as they can manage: "Well, Doctor, is it serious?" we know well enough what they mean. They mean: "Is there any risk of my dying from it?"

Every sickness is a crisis of life. Every sick person who calls for our help is one who has suddenly become aware of his fragility. "What is your life?" says St. James. "For ye are a vapour, that appeareth for a little time, and then vanisheth away" (Jas. 4:14). He is at the same time discovering the fragility of everything that once filled his life: work, money, affections, instincts, and pleasures. If he has regarded them as duties and blessings sent by God, the sudden stoppage caused by the sickness will be easier to bear: he still has God and will wait upon new blessings from him in the spiritual retreat that sickness can become. But if, on the other hand, he has made them his gods, if he has thrown himself frantically into them in order to distract and dope himself, then suddenly and tragically he is faced with the true problems of life. Sickness sets him face to face with God.

Many sick people feel rebellious because they consider their illness to be an unexpected accident which they do not deserve. In the biblical perspective they may come to see the truth that death and disease are a necessary destiny. To put it quite frankly: they are even normal. Here again the Bible is completely realistic.

For affliction cometh not forth of the dust,
Neither doth trouble spring out of the ground;
But man is born unto trouble,
As the sparks fly upward (Job 5:6-7).

The prolonging of life and reestablishing of health, for which medicine labors with all its strength, are a blessing from the merciful God, a stay of execution. We may ask why God grants us this respite. It can only be that he wants us to use it to come nearer to him, laying hold through faith on his promises of eternal life.

True courage—the courage which has its roots in

faith—is that which listens to what God is saying to us through disease and the threat of death. If this is our attitude, sickness and death will take on meaning for us. They will have something to teach us, and will help us to revise our scale of values.

Sin and suffering

The impressive account of Moses' death brings us back to the grave problem of the relationship of disease, death and sin. We read that "his eye was not dim, nor his natural force abated" (Deut. 34:7). Nevertheless God sent him to the top of Mount Nebo to look from afar at the promised land that his people, but not he, would enter. And God said to him: "Die in the mount . . . as Aaron thy brother died . . . because ye trespassed against me in the midst of the children of Israel" (Deut. 32:50-1).

Was not Moses the great servant of God? We are told of him that the Lord knew him face to face (Deut. 34:10). How well the phrase shows the personalism of the Bible! Did he not show himself untiring in God's cause, unbending in his struggles against the people? And yet God announced to Moses his premature death, indicating that it was the price he must pay for sins committed "in the midst of the children of Israel." Did Moses revolt against the injustice of it? Far from it. He sang a glorious song of praise: "Ascribe ye greatness unto our God. He is the Rock, his work is perfect; for all his ways are judgment" (Deut. 32:3-4).

Moses might well have felt himself the innocent victim of that people. In spite of all his courageous striving, the people had repeatedly aroused God's wrath by their rebellions. And now it was he, Moses, who was to be the victim of it.

The greatness of Moses lies in the fact that he had made himself so much one with his people that he could not say: "It is not just, because it is not my fault." The faults of his people, although he never ceased to combat them, he felt to be his responsibility. Vocation implies responsibility. Let me illustrate with a personal experience of my own.

I had had a serious car accident in which my wife and one of our children had been injured. My uncle who had brought me up after the death of my father had been killed. That night my brain turned over and over the feverish thoughts that assailed me. Legally I was not responsible: I was the victim of Fate. There had been a heavy shower, perhaps a patch of oil on the road, and my car had skidded. But I had paid no attention a little while before to a notice warning drivers of the slippery road surface. I was not traveling very fast; but half an hour earlier I had been delighting in my skill in driving at speed.

Above all I felt that all this inner discussion would in no wise bring me peace. Even if I could without reticence have gathered together all the arguments exonerating me from responsibility they would not have exonerated me. I was indeed a victim, but I was to blame as well. If I had been in closer contact with God, more open to his inspiration, he doubtless would have led me so that this thing would not have happened. That very morning, in haste to get away, I had cut short my prayer time; and the prayers I had said had been only an imitation of prayers.

That is sin, to be out of contact with God, to be

separated from him and from his guidance. I realized it is absolutely impossible by intellectual processes to separate that of which we are the victims from that for which we are to blame. It is not a matter for analysis; it is beyond all analysis. And then, in the pleasure I take in driving, I am one with the modern world with its swarms of cars and its patches of oil, increasing the risk of death. I am a part of it, I help to create it, to make it what it is. Like all other men, I am responsible for it as well.

Finally, though we can make amends for some of the wrongs we have done, there are others which are irreparable, particularly when a death has occurred. That night I felt and understood the meaning of the Cross of Christ: that the Cross is the reparation for the irreparable—that we all bear a burden in which we are mingled inextricably. We are the victims and we are to blame, but we can lay down this entire burden just as it is at the foot of the Cross, for the Cross is at the same time forgiveness where we are guilty and relief where we are the victims.

A simple image may help to make this clear. The world is like a great ship on which we are all embarked without having wished to be so and which, from time immemorial, has been disabled. In the beginning, through disobeying the captain's orders, the crew handled the ship badly, and it was holed. Since then, urged on by the instinct of self-preservation, or sometimes by a noble ideal, the crew has been feverishly trying to repair the damage. But the fear and confusion that reign create tumult, and the ship is handled worse than ever so that even constructive efforts result in further damage. The sailors argue about the best method of effecting the repairs and these arguments add to the confusion. The noise of them makes it impossible to hear clearly the captain's orders.

In this ship each one is a victim, a victim of the fateful diabolical chain of events, a victim of the wrongs of others; but each is at fault also and contributes, even with good intentions, his share to the general tumult. And the disaster which threatens each one is bound up with all the disorder. Each feels his responsibility since each must strive to avert it. Yet none can be judged to be more responsible than another.

This was what I realized that night after my accident. It brought me to my knees before the Cross. Was not the meaning of this accident for me just what God had made me realize through it? Since that night I see more clearly the tragedy of human life. I have understood how inexorable it is, and how there is no other help than the grace of God. One of my patients once said that sin can lead only either to despair or to God.

Since that time it has been given to me to serve my fellow men with an ever-deepening understanding of their needs. Men and women of all ages and conditions have come to me bearing a burden made up of that inextricable mixture of guilt and suffering. There are indeed in their lives some things of which they can truthfully say they are the victims and some for which they really feel themselves to blame. But when we look closely at these things we find that the frontier between them is far from being clearly demarcated.

I shall never forget the first words I heard from the mouth of Dr. Maeder of Zurich. He had just been converted to Christianity and was witnessing to his experience: "For more than twenty years I had been caring for men's souls without seeing the most important fact about the life of the soul—namely, sin."

Throughout the Bible the healing of disease is presented as the symbol of God's grace which at the same time purifies the soul of its sin. Thus, while avoiding completely any suggestion of a causal link between the sins and the paralysis of the sick man, Jesus dealt at once with both.

Think of all those sick people who flocked to Jesus. He never repulsed them; he never told them they must first repent. His calls to repentance were directed to everybody and especially to the healthy and the self-satisfied. But with the sick his first care was to afford relief and healing.

There is here a clear lead for the doctor. The patient who comes to him does not want a sermon or an exhortation to repentance, but help in his suffering. The doctor must never be like Job's friend who said to him: "Who ever perished, being innocent?" (Job 4:7). We can well understand Job's vehemence to his friends: "Ye are all physicians of no value" (Job 13:4).

It would be wrong for us ever to speak to our patients of their sin or even to suggest to ourselves that there might be a connection between this sin and their illness. "Charity," says St. Paul, "thinketh no evil" (I Cor. 13:5). If they broach the subject it is another matter. We shall return later to the therapeutic value of confession. On the other hand, when the patient is healed we can often show him that his recovery is a blessing granted by God and turn his thoughts to the new responsibilities that this involves.

In a passage from St. James' Epistle we see once more that double aspect of grace, manifesting itself at the same time in healing and in forgiveness. "Is any among you sick? Let him call for the elders of the church; and let them pray over him, anointing him with oil in the name of the Lord. And the prayer of faith shall save him that is sick, and the Lord shall raise him up; and if he have committed sins, it shall be forgiven him" (Jas. 5:14-15).

The Bible, while affirming the existence of a general connection between sin and affliction, never sees health and prosperity as a measure of holiness or faith. In the biblical perspective all men are sinners: "There is none righteous, no, not one" (Rom. 3:10). He who thinks himself less sinful than his neighbor is further than he from the Kingdom of God, as Jesus shows by his parable of the Pharisee and the Publican (Luke 18:9-14). "The last shall be first, and the first last," He says (Matt. 20:16). Troubles come indifferently to the good and the wicked; God's gifts also are for all. "All things come alike to all," says the Preacher. "There is one event to the righteous and to the wicked" (Eccl. 9:2). And Jesus echoes him: "Your Father . . . maketh his sun to rise on the evil and the good, and sendeth rain on the just and the unjust" (Matt. 5:45).

The spectacle of the "prosperity of the wicked" (Ps. 73:3) exercises many of the biblical writers. "Righteous art thou, O Lord, when I plead with thee," cries Jeremiah, "yet would I reason the cause with thee. Wherefore doth the way of the wicked prosper? Wherefore are all they at ease that deal very treacherously?" (Jer. 12:1) To Jeremiah both the Bible and modern analytical psychology reply that there is wickedness and treachery in the hearts of all men and that none of them lives at ease.

But if we study the Bible honestly we shall come across numerous passages also where a specific affliction—an accident, an illness, a bereavement, a death—is represented as being the direct consequence of a fault or even as a punishment for it.

In the New Testament, mention must be made of the suicide of Judas Iscariot (Matt. 27:5), the death of Ananias and Sapphira (Acts 5:1-11) and in particular a passage in St. Paul. He is stigmatizing the disorders that have crept into the Church in Corinth, where the celebration of the Lord's Supper has been turned into an orgy. He adds: "For this cause many among you are weak and sickly, and not a few sleep" (I Cor. 11:30).

We must see in all these texts the personal witness of men who have become aware of the greatness of God and of the enormity of sin. They are all illustrations of St. Paul's saying: "Be not deceived; God is not mocked" (Gal. 6:7). It is in this sense that they speak to us even if some of them do leave us somewhat uneasy.

The Bible boldly asserts that God suffers in all ills that his children bring down upon themselves by their disobedience: "For he doth not afflict willingly, nor grieve the children of men" (Lam. 3:33).

Here doctors have plenty of testimony to add. They see sick people alight with joy and hear them speak of the wonderful fruits their afflictions have borne. "I had forgotten God, when things were all right with me," one of my patients said to me. The words were simple but they came from the heart. She was echoing Pascal in his prayer for the good use of disease: "Thou didst give me health that I might serve thee, and I put it all to worldly use. Now thou sendest me sickness to correct me; let me not use it to avoid thee through my impatience."

The Apostle James writes: "Count it all joy, my brethren, when ye fall into manifold temptations; knowing that the proof of your faith worketh patience" (Jas. 1:2-3). Have you never found yourself saying of a hardhearted man, "You can see that he has never suffered"?

This seems to be the meaning of suffering, in the Bible, that it is a school of faith. This is the whole message of the Book of Job. "Happy is the man whom God correcteth" (Job 5:17). And the Epistle to the Hebrews quotes Proverbs, "Whom the Lord loveth he chasteneth" (Heb. 12:6; Prov. 3:12), and the Revelation takes up the saying: "As many as I love, I reprove and chasten" (Rev. 3:19). We find it in St. Peter: "You . . . are kept through faith. . . . Wherein ye greatly rejoice, though now for a little while, if need be, ye have been put to grief in manifold trials, that the proof of your faith, being more precious than gold that perisheth though it is proved by fire, might be found unto praise and glory and honor" (I Pet. 1:5-7). And again in St. Paul: "We are pressed on every side, yet not straitened; perplexed, yet not unto despair; pursued, yet not forsaken; smitten down, yet not destroyed . . . for our light affliction, which is for the moment worketh for us more and more exceedingly an eternal weight of glory; while we look not at the things which are seen, but at the things which are not seen" (II Cor. 4:8-9, 17-18).

Finally, our study of the meaning of affliction must bring us again to the subject of death. Beyond and in spite of all we have said, death is clearly thought of in the Bible as a blessing from God.

Think again of the account of the Garden of Eden which we studied earlier. Side by side with the tree of the knowledge of good and evil there also grew "the tree of life" (Gen. 2:9). We are told that God drove Adam from the Garden after the Fall in order to prevent him from touching also the tree of life: "Lest he put forth his hand, and take also of the tree of life, and eat, and live for ever" (Gen. 3:22).

In this life suffering must be relieved, the sick healed, and life prolonged as far as possible, but it is only a temporary expedient. It merely prolongs the suffering. Nothing would be worse than to live in our condition for ever.

This is why we feel ourselves to be "sojourners and pilgrims" on the earth (I Pet. 2:11). As Christians we know that "our citizenship is in heaven" (Phil. 3:20). These are not the words of defeatists. They come from the pens of the Apostles Peter and Paul, energetic builders of the Church.

We are indeed promised eternal life but in a restored world freed from suffering. It is the central theme of our Lord's own teaching and he returns to it constantly. It begins in this life, in so far as he lays hold upon us.

Thus the image of the "tree of life" reappears twice

in the Bible in prophetic visions of the restored world. In the prophet Ezekiel we read, "And by the river upon the bank thereof, on this side and on that side, shall grow every tree for meat, whose leaf shall not wither, neither shall the fruit thereof fail. It shall bring forth new fruit every month . . . and the fruit thereof shall be for meat, and the leaf thereof for healing" (Ezek. 47:12). And in Revelation: "In the midst of the street thereof, and on this side of the river and on that was a tree of life, bearing twelve crops of fruit, yielding its fruit every month, and the leaves of the tree were for the healing of the nations" (Rev. 22:2, R.V. marg.).

So death is a blessing from God. Through it we inherit eternal life in a world where "neither shall there be mourning, nor crying, nor pain any more" (Rev. 21:4). Has not every doctor at some time seen death as a merciful blessing after awful agony?

5
Accepting Life

The Christian response to suffering is acceptance. Through acceptance suffering bears spiritual fruit—and psychic and physical fruit as well.

Resignation is passive. Acceptance is active. Resignation abandons the struggle against suffering. Acceptance strives without backsliding, but also without rebellion.

In a lecture delivered to the German Philosophical Society, the surgeon Sauerbruch declared: "Faith deep-rooted in the soul has more efficacy than all philosophical knowledge. Pain and suffering find their liberating meaning only in the Christian faith."

A psychiatrist told me that he had once been summoned by an old friend whom he had not seen for a number of years, and who also had Parkinson's disease. The sick man had added to the message he sent: "Only come if you have some new remedy to bring. I've had enough of doctors who say they cannot cure me."

As he went into the bedroom the psychiatrist said to his friend: "I've brought you a new remedy—Jesus Christ."

His remark was not at all well received: the patient bitterly reproached his friend for mocking him. But when the psychiatrist had talked of the change brought about in his own life since he had encountered Jesus Christ, the tone of the conversation altered, and the patient opened his heart as well.

The Bible records the life and death of Jesus Christ, the God-man, who knew all our physical, psychic, and spiritual difficulties, and who alone, through his perfect obedience, resolved them all. Living in personal fellowship with him we see what our personal problems are, and above all we find the supernatural strength we need to supplement our own poor efforts to resolve them. We have seen how suffering is often bound up with our disobedience and our wrong modes of life. In order to strive effectively against suffering we must come to Christ, who delivers us from our faults. Through his sacrifice on the Cross, he brings us supreme deliverance, taking upon himself all the wrongs that our efforts have failed to put right, and granting us God's forgiveness.

Despite the most telling spiritual experiences, there subsist in every man's life sufferings which God does not relieve. So to St. Paul, who thrice asked God to remove his "thorn in the flesh," God answered: "My grace is sufficient for you" (II Cor. 12:9).

Accepting suffering, bereavement, and disease does not mean taking pleasure in them, steeling oneself against them, or hoping that distractions or the passage of time will make us forget them. It means offering them to God so that he can make them bring forth fruit. One does not arrive at this through reasoning, nor is it to be understood through logic. It is the experience of the grace of God.

I had an old and dear friend, one of the men I have esteemed most highly. For some weeks his health had been deteriorating. It was on Christmas Day that the doctor who tended him asked me to go with him on what would probably be his last visit.

The patient could speak only with difficulty. Medicine could afford little relief. We concentrated on surrounding the sick man with our affection. I was left alone with him for a moment. He spoke painfully to me: "There's something I don't understand . . ." He did not succeed in saying what it was he did not understand. This struck me particularly because he was a man who all his life had been devoted to intellectual clarity. Faith had always had the last word with him, but it was allied to a most lively intelligence. One felt that he was still troubled by whatever it was he did not understand. But he was too weak now to put his problem into words. And I realized that it would have been useless to ask him any questions, or to start a discussion.

After a moment's silence, I bent over him and said quietly: "You know that the most important thing in this world is not to understand, but to accept." With a happy smile he stammered: "Yes . . . it's true . . . I do accept . . . everything." It was almost the last thing he said. After my visit he fell asleep. During the night he suddenly awoke, sat up, and said, "I am going to heaven." Then he died.

The Christian message of acceptance is not an answer only to exceptional suffering. It applies to hundreds of aspects of daily life. Acceptance of living is one of the most important factors in healing.

Acceptance of growing old means living in the present, at any age, even if the past has been rich in beautiful experiences. During a visit to one of my patients I admired the flowers on her balcony. But there were some faded flowers among them, and I said to her: "You must cut off the faded flowers so that the plant will grow new ones." I realized at once that this was a parable of life. The flowers were beautiful once, but time passes and if we try to preserve the flowers of the past we have only faded flowers on our plant, and prevent it from producing new ones.

Parents, too, must accept their children. There are many parents who are disappointed in their children because the children do not fit into the fine pattern they had dreamed of. There are many children who feel vaguely oppressed by this undefined parental disapproval. Accepting one's children means accepting their temperaments, their failings, their character, and sex.

Accepting one's life means accepting all that one considers to be unfair victimization, the injustices of fate as well as those of men. We sometimes say that we would be willing to accept the injustices provided that at least we were asked to forgive them. But the Christian is required to forgive even those who do not ask for forgiveness.

Accepting one's life means also accepting the sin of others which causes us suffering. Accepting their nerves, their reactions, their enthusiasms, and even the talents and qualities by means of which they outshine us. It means accepting our families, our clients, our fellow workers, our place in society, our country.

Unless one has accepted one's work, one does it halfheartedly and remains dissatisfied with the result. It is also much more tiring. I am reminded of a young woman who lost weight while at work, and put it on again during holidays with astonishing rapidity. When we looked more closely into the situation we realized that what was damaging her health was not so much the work itself as the wearing effect of a constant revolt against that particular work.

Many people will not accept their own bodies. No one knows the secret torment, often childish, but capable of turning into a regular obsession, that can be caused by a nose that is too long, legs that are too thick, by being too tall or too short, by a tendency to plumpness, or an unharmonious voice—in short, by revolt against not being as handsome or as beautiful as one would like. What fixes these preoccupations, and makes them worse, is the very fact that they are secret. If such worries were openly voiced, reassurance might be forthcoming from the person's friends, and he might be quite astonished to learn that his little physical defects are hardly noticed and that his friends appreciate his other and more important qualities.

Accepting one's physical make-up means that one will stop comparing oneself with others. My wife is delicate, while I am a man of action.One day during her meditation she came to see that God's purpose for her was different from his purpose for me. what he required from her was an account of her own talent, and not of mine. That was the beginning of a great development in her as a person.

Happiness, inner harmony, acceptance of our

lives, the solving of conflicts with others, satisfaction in work, victory over sin, idleness, and selfishness have doubtless more influence on our vitality than all the other physical factors of diet, heredity, constitution, or rest. They constitute a sort of coefficient which multiplies the basic figure of physical vitality.

Acceptance of one's marriage partner means acceptance of one's wife as she is and acceptance of one's husband as he is. Further, accepting one's marriage partner involves real acceptance of marriage itself. There are more married people than one would think who are not totally married. They have mental or emotional reservations. They do not accept the restrictions which marriage imposes on their liberty. They wish to go their own way and enjoy their own amusements and to spend their money as they like.

The first prerequisite of Christian marriage is that the man and the woman should have been brought together by God.

Next in importance is that the engagement should be in conformity with God's purpose. The happiness of many a marriage is spoiled by unchastity and selfishness during the engagement.

Last, it is vital that the union should be submitted to the authority of God. Both partners must seek to establish spiritual communion. The dictates of the Scriptures should govern their attitude to each other, every difficulty being resolved through prayer. The home must find its meaning in service together of God.

As we have said earlier, there is nothing wrong with the sex instinct. What is sinful is its use outside what God meant it to be. Without God, the regulation of the sex life in marriage is either a compromise in which each partner hides his real thoughts from the other, or a tyranny by one over the other. Or it may be an artificial and rigid edifice of formal principles. No moral or psychological system can regulate by principles a domain which belongs to daily obedience to God, to the free submission to him of the conscience enlightened by the Scriptures and the teaching of the church. When God directs the sex life of a married couple, they can practice it divinely, if I may use the word—in a full mutual communion that is carnal, moral, and spiritual all at once. It is the crowning symbol of their total giving of themselves to each other.

Many parents and educators who generally have not themselves succeeded in resolving their own sex problems think they are helping young people by parading before them the specter of the supposedly terrible results of masturbation. These young people then get bogged down in a negative and obsessive struggle. They come to isolate this problem from other personal problems, such as that of not having a frank and loving relationship with their parents. The reader must understand that I am not advocating here anything but a high ideal of purity in young people. But what I maintain is that the struggle for this ideal is effective only when it takes its place in the framework of a total consecration of one's life to Jesus Christ, and when obedience to him in all other respects concerns the young person as much as his sexual continence.

A positive struggle counts on the supernatural strength which Christ gives to those who dedicate the whole of their lives to him. I know a young man who when he was tempted, instead of bracing himself stiffly in a negative effort, would get down on his knees and thank God for having placed in him such a life-force, and ask him how he ought to use it.

The biblical message of acceptance is the only possible answer to the great problem of suffering.

From the miracles that are wrought through acceptance it can be seen that spiritual strength is the greatest strength in the world. It alone can insure victory over the negative forces of selfishness, hate, fear, and disorder, which destroy peoples and undermine the health of individuals. It alone gives them the joy, energy, and zeal needed in the daily battle for life and for the defense of health.

Health is not the mere absence of disease. It is a quality of life, a physical, psychical, and spiritual unfolding, an exaltation of personal dynamism.

6
The Doctor's Mission

Mlle. S. Fouche of Paris, who has devoted her life to the rehabilitation of the crippled and the sick, made an investigation among two hundred patients of what they expected from the doctor. When I heard their replies read I was deeply moved. The men were more realistic than the women. What they expected foremost from the doctor was to be cured. But in all the replies three themes reappeared with striking urgency and regularity. They wanted the doctor to pay real attention to their suffering and distress, to treat them as human beings and not as guinea pigs, and to tell them the truth about their disease and its probable duration. But many of them added that they did not want the truth to be told them brutally, so that they were cowed and shocked by it, but gently and tactfully so that they might be helped to accept it.

I must confess that I have not always been able to tell a patient seriously ill what I thought about his condition. I have always felt that my fault lay farther back, that it was less in this silence, which was after all imposed by charity, than in not having been able earlier, when the patient was not so near death, to establish close contact with him and to create that climate of spiritual fellowship without which the truth cannot be told. It is in speaking of the meaning of things that we enter into this fellowship, giving the patient an opportunity of talking to us about the things that are weighing on his mind, long before he has reached the last extremity.

There is a streak of cowardice in all of us, doctors and patients alike. Each one of us, and more strongly than we care to confess, puts up a stubborn resistance against tackling the problems of suffering, disease and death. It inevitably brings up problems in which the doctor himself is often in the dark. There are many doctors who hold high professional ideals, who long with all their hearts to practice a humane medicine. But can they without a religious faith? For if they are not fully convinced that their own life has a meaning, how can they approach the questions their patients put to them about human destiny? It is then that they are so easily tempted to change the subject of conversation. All they need to do is to admire the bunch of carnations on the table, or to talk of some X-ray photograph from which they are expecting to get valuable information. The awkward discussion which the patient desires and which the doctor fears is avoided.

When the disease is not serious, it is easy to avoid the problem of death and to keep up morale by assuring the patient of his recovery. And if the condition of the patient worsens it will be perhaps too late, too difficult.

Disease does not always end in cure or in death. It may be prolonged and become chronic or it may leave behind it a permanent infirmity.

When the doctor can do no more to heal, his task is not over. It is much more difficult and thankless but just as necessary. He has to help the cripple to accept the inevitable and to engage in the struggle to adapt himself so that he is not allowed to lose his share in the life of the community. It is often thought that these two things are incompatible—that the cripple who accepts his infirmity must cease the struggle for reintegration and that to fight must mean to revolt against the infirmity. Experience proves otherwise. If the cripple revolts and complains he cripples his spirit also and shuts himself off from outside contacts, becoming hard and inadaptable. But in so far as he succeeds, helped by his faith in accepting his infirmity, he relaxes and finds in himself new energy to live in spite of everything, and often an extraordinary capacity to overcome his difficulties.

In cases of chronic disease the patient expects us to share in his sufferings, traveling with him in it faithfully to the end. He wants us to help him to live notwithstanding, and to help him to die. That seems to me to sum up the whole of medicine—helping men to live and to die.

A few days ago the medical superintendent of a large sanatorium said, "Just think how hard it is to come day after day for weeks and months to the bedside of some of those in the ward without ever being able to bring them good news or to suggest for them the operation whose success they can see in others around them." How great is the temptation to space out one's visits in order to avoid these painful interviews or else to do what I call playing tricks, to affect humor or artificial high spirits, to make small talk so as to crowd out more serious topics. The chronic invalid is very sensitive. Such tricks do not deceive him. The invalids who are always complaining are almost easier to deal with for they provoke an active reaction, but the gentle ones, whose eyes only ask their unspoken questions—how hard it is to face for long the infinite confidence of their gaze.

Everything that I have said regarding chronic invalids and the infirm is true also of neurotics, whose treatment is so often long-drawn-out. It is easy to sympathize on our first contact, to penetrate wholeheartedly the neurotic's life problems, to share his feelings in the shocks he has suffered and which have made him the invalid he is. But when relief is slow in coming, it becomes a heavy burden to bear. It is not the patient who is burdensome; it is the disease. But he is quick to think that it is he who is weighing on us and not his ills!

The other day I was overjoyed to see a woman whom I treated for ten years for most distressing neurotic obsessions. She was always afraid that I should weary of her; she even blamed herself for not being able to bring me success to crown my efforts on her behalf. Then suddenly one Good Friday the thing happened. She felt that she had been sent peace and the anxiety disappeared. An interesting medical detail in this case is that the psychological trouble was accompanied by physical disturbance, in particular a stubborn condition of anemia. Throughout all those years preparations of iron or of liver extract had never succeeded in raising the level of hemoglobin above 55 percent. Now it is a fact that three weeks after the final disappearance of the psychological symptoms and without her having undergone any further anti-anemic treatment the hemoglobin level was found to be 78 percent.

But technical treatment and human sympathy are not enough. The mission of the doctor is wider still. Helping a person to live does not mean only helping him to bear his life but helping him to grow and to solve his problems. Every disease compels the patient to turn in upon himself and to examine his life, and for this also he needs his doctor. If sickness in general is a sign of our frailty, of the disorder that has broken into the world, and of our moral nature, each particular case of sickness has its own peculiar meaning.

Job saw his sickness as a test through which God sought to strengthen his faith (Jas. 5:11). St. Paul saw his as a thorn in the flesh which God would not remove in order to keep him from pride, so that in his weakness he would rely only on God's strength (II Cor. 12:7).

As soon as we begin to listen to the confidences of our patients, we find that they discover something about the meaning of their illness. This is especially so in the case of neuroses. One of my patients once said to me: "I see now that I shall never be cured of my neurosis until I have learned what God is seeking to teach me through it."

One further case, a man suffering from furunculosis. He was soon able to confess to me that the boils were a physical expression of all the bitterness he was nursing in his soul as a result of repeated quarrels with his wife.

Disease frequently seems to be aimed at a definite end, even though the sufferer may be unaware of it. I am not thinking only of the "flight into disease" in which the patient is trying to win the affection he does not receive when well. There are more subtle cases. Take, for instance, that of a man who in childhood suffered from his father's failure in business and the social discredit which this brought upon the family. From then on a fierce will to succeed in life took hold of him and spurred him on to climb all the rungs of promotion in the firm he had joined. At last the long-awaited day came when he was appointed its director. That very day he fell seriously ill. But that illness has borne unexpected fruit. He sees now that he was the unconscious victim of this personal will to success which possessed and enslaved him and whose power has at last been broken by his illness. Through it he has become aware that ever since his childhood God has been calling him to give up to him this will of his. And now, instead of fighting God's call, he is able to respond to it.

A few days ago a workman engaged in the construction of a garage for the house next door rang my doorbell. He had cut his hand with a saw. Disinfectant, a couple of stitches and a dressing—what could be simpler? It was an almost automatic routine. But we chatted while I was busy: "Have you seen those planks that the boss is making us saw up?" the injured man asked. "They've come straight off the trees; they're so wet it's practically impossible to do anything with them." So in that unfortunate saw cut there was something other than a mere accident. There was the man's irritation with his employer.

When we are irritated by our work our efforts become uncoordinated and jerky—and thus the accident had happened.

It is clear that every illness and every accident reveal problems, sometimes of vital importance, in which physical, psychological and spiritual factors are closely interwoven. We must remember that man is an indivisible unity, and so the vocation of the doctor and that of the pastor cannot be kept in watertight compartments. The same is true in connection with the respective spheres of the doctor and the teacher. Sometimes the doctor may exercise a profound influence on his patient by a straightforward declaration of his faith. A declaration will have more effect than if it came from a clergyman. Let us be frank about this. Problems of the sort we have been discussing in connection with cripples, chronic invalids, neurotics and others who are suffering from life's harshest blows can find a solution only in Christian faith. Thus a verse from the Bible may afford real relief—and the only true relief—like, for example, that in which the prophet Isaiah anticipates Christ's succor: "Surely he hath borne our griefs, and carried our sorrows" (Isa. 53:4).

But we do not have to be continually talking about God. I am reminded of a patient who turned to me on the doorstep and said: "Doctor, I'm grateful to you for having put God into my life."

"But I can't remember ever having discussed the subject with you," I replied.

"That's true," he said. "But I still feel that it is the result of our talks together."

A married couple came to consult me about their

marital difficulties. I saw either one or the other or both together many times. I became passionately interested in the psychological problems which underlay their difficulties. One day the wife, while staying abroad with some friends, happened to pick up one of my books and learned that I was a Christian, a matter on which I had had no occasion to speak to her. She began to read the Bible and underwent a real conversion. When she came back it was to bring me a confession of her faults and almost to blame me for not having spoken to her before of the Christian life she was now discovering.

We doctors are not called upon by God to preach. Our task is rather to listen and to understand. If we give our patients an opportunity of speaking of what is in their hearts they will get to know themselves better; they will discover what are the real problems they have to face, and perhaps see the meaning of their sickness.

But what are we to do, faced with this flood of problems to which science has no answer and which exhortation does not suffice to resolve? I think that the best thing to do is to speak to our patients about our own experiences, our own difficulties, faults and failures, and about the blessings we have received. We should not, of course, overdo all this, but follow that just measure to which God prompts us. In this way, speaking from the heart, we set up that reciprocity which the Bible teaches. The Bible contains much teaching and exhortation; but it contains even more of personal experiences.

We should know nothing of that searching hour spent by Moses (Ex. 3:4) at the beginning of his ministry, when God spoke to him out of the burning bush, if he himself had not spoken of it. He told how he tried to resist God and all the objections he put forward before giving in to his call. We should know nothing of the prophet Isaiah's radical experience when he received his commission from God if he had not told us himself how he became aware of his own sin, and knew that God was purifying him. So even Jesus Christ told of his experiences and his struggles. He told his disciples of his anguish before the Cross: "My soul is exceeding sorrowful, even unto death" (Matt. 26:38).

If, following the example of these, we speak from our hearts, we help our patients to understand their illness. But it is still they themselves that make the discovery.

Professor Courvoisier writes that the vocation of medicine is "a service to which those are called who through their studies and the natural gifts with which the Creator has endowed them . . . are specially fitted to tend the sick and to heal them. Whether or not they are aware of it, whether or not they are believers, this is from the Christian point of view fundamental, that doctors are by their profession fellow workers with God. . . . because their activity is itself a sign of God's patience. It is not his will that men should be lost but that they should all come to the knowledge of his Son and of his salvation."

Thus every doctor, Christian or not, is a collaborator with God. As Ambroise Pare said in these well-known words: "I tended him. God healed him." To know ourselves to be called by God is to believe in our vocation with as much conviction as St. Paul when he declares himself to be "separated unto the gospel of God" (Rom. 1:1). And it is St. Paul who speaks of the "diversities of ministrations" (I Cor. 12:5).

7
Being Honest With Ourselves

The theory of the contraction of the field of consciousness, which we owe to Pierre Janet, and which has been developed by the psychoanalytical school, provides the best explanation of neurosis. These psychologists have shown that when a deep-seated tendency opposed to the moral ideal of the subject makes its presence felt within him, or shows itself through actions of which his conscience disapproves, the memory of these guilty feelings or acts is driven out of the field of consciousness. Later these repressed tendencies and memories reappear, disguised in the form of mental pictures, dreams, bungled actions, or as neurotic symptoms, paralyses, functional disorders, obsessions, and so on.

This doctrine is in full accord with Christian teaching on the human personality. The only difference is that Christianity calls these "deep-seated tendencies opposed to the moral ideal of the subject" simply sin. The Bible shows that man naturally tends to shut his eyes to his faults and to his sufferings. He tends to eliminate from the field of his consciousness any thoughts, memories, events, or temptations connected with sin. Christ, quoting the words of the prophet Isaiah, speaks of the eyes which do not see, the ears which do not hear, and the hearts which do not understand (Mark 8:17-18). The contraction of the field of consciousness could hardly be more clearly described.

The better a man succeeds in becoming honest with himself, the more clearly he will see his field of consciousness expand. When a man meditates in the presence of God, he learns once more how to look his faults in the face. There takes place within him an expansion of the field of consciousness comparable to that obtained by Janet using hypnosis, and by Freud using the analysis of dreams and bungled actions. In Christian soul healing I always feel that I am accompanying my patient on a tour of his mind. He ventures into it as into a darkened room: At first nothing is visible, and then gradually one begins to make out shapeless masses—particular problems. Slowly these masses take on more definite outlines and begin to show detail, until, by the light of Jesus Christ, the mind is known.

Science studies man from without. Meditation which is thought guided by God reveals him from within. We see then how often the conscious and the unconscious counterbalance each other; a conscious virtue hides an unconscious failing. We find that the true motives of our behavior are less flattering than we think, and we see that we are the brothers of all sinners and of all the sick. We discover that in ourselves there are repressed ideas, pretenses, deceit, and fears just like those of our patients, and we can help to free them from them. I strike my dog because he has been disobedient. But when I consider this during my meditation, I realize that I was annoyed with my wife because of a remark she had made to me, and which at the time I pretended to accept, when in fact I had not accepted it. As soon as I make this discovery and write it down in my notebook, or tell my wife about it and ask her to forgive me, I perceive that I already knew of it, but did not dare to admit it clearly to myself. Meditation was needed before I could become aware of what I already knew.

Those who find meditation hardest to practice are the intellectuals. They are assailed by doubts, and wonder if their thoughts are coming from God; whereas a manual laborer, for example, will set down right away on his paper everything that comes into his mind. Then he sees that it is so true, so concrete, and so forthright that he cannot doubt that it comes from God.

Similarly, in meditation, among the thousands of possible associations of ideas, God guides our minds toward certain associations which our complexes (that is to say, our sin) would have prevented us making in any other circumstances. There is therefore no contradiction between psychological determinism and guidance by God of the mind in meditation.

Nothing is better for the mind than a few days spent in solitude and devoted entirely to meditation and to the pooling of thoughts discovered in this way. My wife and I have done this several times. It is the best kind of holiday, the most luminous days it is possible to live through. It is also the profoundest way for a married couple to get to know each other.

True love often makes us see in those we love failings we never noticed when we did not care about them. And so we must go back to what Jesus said. He does not deny that there is a speck in our brother's eye, nor that it may be a charitable act to try and get it out for him. He simply tells us to consider first the log in our own eye; that is to say, to direct the searchlight of our field of consciousness upon ourselves. The more clearly we learn to see our own faults, the freer shall we be from the spirit of criticism.

Thus through the repentance and forgiveness to which it leads, Christian soul healing provides the answer to all the disorders of the field of consciousness: contraction, expansion in respect of other people, expansion in respect of oneself, and displacement.

But it brings furthermore a quite different kind of succor to the troubled mind, a succor whose effect is synthesis. I have mentioned the danger of overdoing self-analysis. The safeguard against this danger is to "Overcome evil with good" (Rom. 12:21), and in doing so Paul invites those who are getting lost in the labyrinth of self-analysis to turn their eyes away toward the positive call of the gospel of Jesus Christ.

"Forgetting what lies behind, and straining forward to what lies ahead, I press on toward the goal," writes St. Paul again (Phil. 3:13-14). Conscious of God's forgiveness, the mind, without going analytically into all the remote factors in its difficulties, can resolve them all by making the leap of faith. It abandons the fruitless search into the past, and the empty analysis of the present, and can turn its thoughts toward action.

In the practice of spiritual meditation one becomes able to see clearly into one's own mind, but one also learns to see more clearly what it is that God is expecting one to do. A young man once told me of a conversation he had had the day before with a friend. As he was speaking to him about looking for God's will in meditation, his friend interrupted him with these words: "What you call God, I call my conscience."

"Our conscience tells us what we must not do," the young man replied, "but God tells us what we must do."

God has a plan for each one of us. He has prepared us for it by means of the particular gifts and temperament he has given to each of us. To discern this plan through seeking day by day to know his will is to find the purpose of our lives. Having an aim in life is a fundamental condition of physical, moral, and spiritual health.

A conviction of vocation—any vocation—is a real motive force in a person's life, ensuring full physical development and psychic equilibrium.

One who has submitted his life to God's authority does not look to him for guidance only when he has some great decision, such as the choice of a career, or a wife. Day by day he finds in meditation fresh inspiration for his daily work, his personal behavior, and his attitude toward those about him. I have given a number of examples of this in the course of this book. My experience is that when God's guidance is sought in this way, those conditions of life which are not favorable to health are generally established. We still make frequent mistakes over what God is expecting of us; we often take our own inclinations for a divine call; we still frequently disobey. And yet, if we remain loyal, we become more and more able to see our own errors, and are more faithful in correcting them.

A diet governed by God, and not by gluttony or fashion; sleep, rest, and holidays dictated by God, and not by laziness or selfishness; a career, work, and physical recreation guided by God, and not by ambition or fear; a marriage and family life directed by God, and not by the desire for personal gratification or by jealousy; personal discipline in the use of our time, in imagination and thoughts, imposed by God and not by caprice or the need to escape—these are the fundamental conditions of both physical and psychical health.

In the Bible are numerous accounts of persons who believed in the will of God, who sought to know and to follow it even in the smallest details of their personal lives. They knew how to listen to God's voice and obey him, sought to know what God wanted them to say, where he wanted them to go, and what he wanted them to do. All the books of the Prophets, and that of the Acts of the Apostles, are pictures of lives guided by God. The Gospels show Jesus Christ meditating and fasting in the desert, fighting against the temptations of the Devil, and seeking God's inspiration for his ministry. They show him going away by himself in the early morning to meet God face to face and to receive his orders for the day's work. They show him constantly escaping from the flattery of men and their worldly requests, to continue on his way from place to place, in accordance with God's plan. They show him, on the eve of the Passion, withdrawing with his disciples, at Caesarea Philippi, and hearing God's call to go up to Jerusalem to suffer and to die there, and telling his disciples of his decision. They show him in the Garden of Gethsemane, still seeking to follow God's will rather than his own.

And throughout the church's history, all the saints who have exerted a profound influence on humanity have been men and women who, breaking away from the conventions of society, and even from the customs of church people, have obeyed God's commands—commands which their contemporaries often failed to understand.

The Christian life does not consist in being perfect, much less in claiming to be so. On the contrary, it consists in being honest about one's shortcomings so as to be able to turn to Jesus Christ for forgiveness and liberation.

This is why I feel that the deepest meaning of medicine is still not in "counseling lives," but in leading the sick to this personal encounter with Jesus Christ.

Advice acts from without. The spiritual revolution takes place within. When a man encounters Jesus Christ, he feels all at once that he has been freed from some passion or some habit to which he has been enslaved, from some fear or rancor against which he has deployed his stoutest efforts in vain.

To seek in prayer the purpose of God for our lives, and to enjoy personal fellowship with Jesus Christ who delivers us from the things that stand in the way of that purpose, leads to that harmony of the whole person which is one of the prerequisites of health.

The Christian experience is the breaking in of Jesus Christ into a person's life, bringing relaxation of tension, confidence, and a new liberating force. Legalism, on the other hand, means slavery to "principles" and continual efforts to satisfy the imperious demands of a moral code.

True liberation through Jesus Christ, however, is a very rare thing. It is in order to hide from himself his lack of real experience that the religious person so often pretends to be freed from sins and passions from which he has not, in fact, been delivered. This lack of sincerity with himself sets up a conflict in him. The doctor sees plenty of these religious people, ravaged by inextricable inner conflicts. The man in the street does not need to be a psychologist to sense this fact, and he simply says that he has no desire to be like them.

Nothing is further from the spirit of Christ than exhorting a person sick in mind to make an effort of will of which he is incapable. On the other hand, to lead him into personal contact with Jesus Christ will be to help him to find the supernatural strength which will bring him victories his own efforts could never have won for him.

It is no light matter to struggle against sin! It is not sufficient to urge people to mend their ways, to point out the price that has to be paid for men's faults, to denounce the modern decline in moral standards. No power will stem the power of sin apart from that of Jesus Christ himself.

I cannot conclude a book in which I have shown the favorable consequences to health of a specifically Christian experience without touching upon questions which more than one reader, no doubt, would like to put to me: Are there not some mental disorders which are actually brought about by a religious experience? Are not some patients who believe they have had a spiritual experience of this kind simply the victims of mental disorders?" Yes, of course; that is incontestable. I side unequivocally with the Rev. Fr. De Sinety, who maintains that no greater disservice can be done to the cause of Christianity than to deny that pathological disorders can simulate genuine religious experience. But he points out that the fact that there are pseudo-mystics does not give us the right to deny that there are real ones.

The same is true of miraculous cures, which I have intentionally bypassed, because they are rather a special case among the subjects that have a bearing on the relationship between medicine and religion. We have no right to deny that miraculous cures do sometimes take place, simply because a large number that are claimed as miraculous can be shown to be merely the result of psychological suggestion.

Finally, it is only right for me to say that I could report several cases where I have been called upon to deal with serious mental disorders that have made their appearance following religious experiences, particularly meetings for witness. I have several times had to have such people sent to mental institutions.

Spiritual power is the greatest power in the world. Although, in order to shake a person out of his state of self-satisfaction, make him look at himself properly, and draw him out of the fortress of compromise in which he has taken refuge from an unquiet conscience, it is often necessary to subject him to the intense emotion of long spiritual retreats, this same power can in others spark serious mental accidents. Such accidents are in fact a proof of the power of the spiritual, just as medicinal intoxication is a proof of the pharmaco-dynamics of medicines. All around us there are people whose psychological equilibrium is so unstable that they are ready to burst out at any moment. Any emotional shock—bereavement, being thwarted, or even a physical disease—can spark a conflagration. It is not surprising therefore that experiences touching on a subject as emotionally charged as religion should also be capable of provoking it.

Does this mean that neurotics ought to be kept away from the message of Christianity? What I said just now about the pharmaco-dynamics of medicines seems to me to provide the answer to this question. The same message which when delivered too abruptly and wholesale may provoke mental disorders, may also, when given in proper doses, be a healing agent. The unstable equilibrium of a person with neurotic tendencies is made up of countless compromises; nevertheless it is an equilibrium. A total decision for Christ is capable of producing a better equilibrium. But such a decision first reopens so many unresolved problems that there is a critical zone to cross.

To be religious one does not have to be simple-minded. It does not help neurotics if we are taken in by their facile spiritual enthusiasms. Charity demands that we be severe and realistic with neurotics, that we should always be bringing them back to the concrete problems of their lives, that we should not be content with anything but a patient effort to solve these problems, denouncing every unconscious attempt to escape in the direction of some easy mystical mirage, and helping them to put into practice, little by little, each new glimpse of God's will for them. There are many people—both among believers and among those who use this as an argument against the Christian faith—who make the mistake of thinking that the Christian must necessarily be naive. Jesus showed himself a true realist when he said that his disciples would be recognizable not by what they said but by the quality of their lives, like a tree by its fruit. We betray the spiritual cause if we allow ourselves to be deceived by people who think their lives have changed because their state of mind has changed, without any real fruit being borne in their daily lives. I could record here many sad cases of neuropaths, especially those of cycloid personality type, who, following upon a theological discussion with a believer—very frequently belonging to one of the Protestant sects—have thought they "understood everything," and have made much of a "conversion" which actually has been purely intellectual. What in fact has happened is that their humor has oscillated from pessimism to optimism, but it is as unreal as it was before. I do not question their sincerity, nor that of those who have communicated to them their theological thoughts. But with those who suffer from nervous disorders one cannot be too realistic, nor too severe in demanding that every new discovery in the realm of the spirit be accompanied by concrete acts of obedience. When one has oneself experienced conversion, one knows what inner battles are involved. One no longer underestimates sin's powers of resistance, and one stresses that the Christian answer is the most costly of all.

I am reminded of one of my patients whose life was a skein of problems of all kinds. In our first interview she told me that she wanted to follow the way of the Christian life. I told her at once that such a decision was valueless and would only lead to disappointments unless she undertook at once courageously to measure the full consequences of it. And I sent her, that same day, to see a young woman who had the patience to devote her whole time to her for four days running, until my patient had written the letters of apology and put into effect the practical decisions necessary to create a new climate in her life.

Faith is not a matter of feeling. For fear of seeming neurotic, many people refrain all their lives from making any affirmation of their faith. They are afraid of religious psychosis. They are afraid of becoming enthusiastic only to be disillusioned later on.

They have not yet realized that true Christianity does not in fact consist of unreal flights of fancy, but of quite concrete experiences.

There are three roads in front of every man: reality without God, which is the dissociation of the materialists; God without reality, which is the dissociation of the pseudo-mystics; and, lastly, God with reality, which is the Christian faith.

This last is the hardest of the three. For it is far easier to live life as we find it, remaining deaf to God's call; or else to answer his call sentimentally, while closing one's eyes to reality. It is easier to be either a materialist or an idealist. What is difficult is to be a Christian.

I come back here to the point from which I started this book, that men's lives are full of concrete problems, material as well as psychological. A religious conversion which avoids these problems, leaving them unresolved, is what too often brings Christianity into disrepute. But a conversion which brings the solution of the problems in a person's life is living proof of the power of Christ.